MODERN FANTASY:
The Hundred Best Novels

By the same author

Science Fiction: The 100 Best Novels
Imaginary People: A Who's Who of Modern Fictional
Characters

MODERN FANTASY

The Hundred Best Novels

An English-Language Selection,
1946–1987

DAVID PRINGLE

PETER BEDRICK BOOKS

NEW YORK

First American edition published in 1989 by
Peter Bedrick Books, New York
by agreement with Grafton Books, a Division of the
Collins Publishing Group, London

©David Pringle 1988

Library of Congress Cataloging-in-Publication Data
Pringle, David.
Modern fantasy: the hundred best novels: an English language
selection, 1946-1987/David Pringle.—1st American ed.
p. ca.
Reprint. Originally published: London: Grafton Books, 1988.
Bibliography: p.
Includes index.
ISBN 0-87226-328-2—ISBN 0-87226-219-7 (pbk.)
1. Fantastic fiction. American—Stories, plots, etc. 2. Fantastic
fiction, English—Stories, plots, etc. 3. Bibliography—Best
books—Fantastic fiction. 4. Fantastic fiction—Bibliography. I.
Title.
PS374.F27P7   1989
813'.0876609—dc20
89-33072
CIP

Manufactured in the United States of America

The paper used in this book complies with the Permanent
Paper Standard issued by the National Information Stan-
dards Organization (Z39.48-1984).

10 9 8 7 6 5 4 3 2 1

FOREWORD

by Brian Aldiss

This is a timely, or at the least, a trendy volume. As David
Pringle says, some impalpable tide has turned in the realm of
reading, and category fantasy is in. Perhaps such fantasy is, as
Pringle amusingly declares, a swamp; if that's so, this guide is
much needed.

And possibly more than a guide, a champion. Fantasy may be
as old as literature and older than the novel; it has certainly been
derided as long as there have been novels, and remains stubbornly
a non-canonical form, perhaps to its own benefit. Even the great
precursor of the novel form, Cervantes' *Don Quixote*, owes its
existence to an intention to deride romances of the Age of
Chivalry. In the bewildered imagination of Cervantes' old knight,
ordinary objects assume fearful and fantastical forms; because of
his reading, he cannot see the world straight.

Similar cautionary tales came later. Jane Austen mocks the
Gothick in *Northanger Abbey*. Charlotte Lennox in *The Female
Quixote* follows Cervantes with her poor Arabella: 'Supposing
Romances were real Pictures of Life, from them she drew all her
Notions and Expectations.' Fantasy distorts: this is the charge
against it.

Yet fantasy proliferates. In an age where we are becoming
statistics and mere consumers, it draws our attention to the drama
of the inner life. And herein lies the key to its febrile attraction:
conservative though most fantasy is by nature, its heroes and
heroines struggling generally to do no more than retain a status
quo, it rejects the profit motive. Beyond the world of the
marketplace, fantasy loiters impecuniously by its swamp, dressed
for the most part merely in gaudy paperback garb. Without a
bean.

In all of Pringle's hundred golden instances, there's not one
central character who has a penny in his pocket. Fantasy not only
turns its back on science and reality: much more determinedly, it

1

rejects the world of finance. Its denizens haven't a cent. Well, there's one character who is so rich he gives money away. Other characters throw up their jobs, their security. Some are actually dead, and so for ever beyond the necessity for credit. Vampires use a different coinage.

That old escapologist, Robert Heinlein, understands the point well. His hero in *Glory Road* escapes into a world where there is 'no Foreign Aid, no hidden taxes – no income tax'.

Not that money is needed in many of these extraordinary worlds of escape. Turn up naked or in pyjamas, you'll make out. Here in never-never-land, the banks have turned into palaces; that's not Wall Street but Gormenghast; Conan clobbered Mammon.

Far future, far past, another dimension: currency is not a problem. It's only in our bloody twentieth century that you have to work for a living. In Elsewhere, you don't need it. Come on, what would Angela Carter's community of tattooed centaurs, or the Torrance family snowed up in Stephen King's lugubrious hotel, or Jack Williamson's beautiful April Bell, transformed into a white wolf, do with dough? This is the great secret freedom of fantasy – that success is not calculated in monetary terms once you escape from the Lands of Almighty Dolour.

It would show discourtesy to be invited into this book and then to quarrel with its interior décor. All the same, as I stand shuffling in the hall, I have an experience which will be common to all visitors: less than total agreement with mine host. Of course. That's inevitable. The swamp is wide, taste subjective in the main.

All the same, I would have liked to see that marvellous fantasy by the early William Golding, *The Inheritors* (told by a Neanderthal), in place of his *Pincher Martin* – indeed, in place of almost anything. And I believe that Stephen Donaldson's work merits much higher praise; there are astonishing revelations in his Thomas Covenant novels, based on a searching moral outlook on life.

And if I were allowed to choose a No. 101 for the year of this elegant guide's first publication, I would go immediately for Doris Lessing's *The Fifth Child*, brilliant, concise, centring on a tormented creature which seems to emerge from the swamp of our own secret imaginings.

Brian W. Aldiss

CONTENTS

NOTE

Cross-reference numbers in italics following
titles in the text refer to the entries
as numbered above.

For my brothers –
Allan, Leslie and Michael

ACKNOWLEDGEMENTS

Many friends and acquaintances have influenced the selection of fantasy novels which follows, although the final choice of titles is mine. I should particularly like to thank Ken Brown, John Clute, Joyce Day and the SF Foundation Library, Mike Dickinson, Gregory Feeley, Joe Hirst, Stephen Jones, Paul Kincaid, Phyllis McDonald, Roger Peyton and Andy Robertson for all their useful suggestions (and, in some cases, the loan of books).

INTRODUCTION

Perhaps we have always enjoyed reading tales of impossible things. But over the past few decades, Fantasy – which is to say, a body of stories that deals in the marvellous, the magical and the otherworldly – has become a highly visible category of prose fiction. The word is now used by publishers, quite unashamedly, on dust-jackets and paperback covers – to such an extent that Fantasy has come to be an accepted genre, like Crime Stories, Romances, Historicals or Thrillers. British and American bookshops, and even best-seller lists, are filled with the stuff (January 1988 top sellers in Britain included such titles as *The Eyes of the Dragon* by Stephen King and *Weaveworld* by Clive Barker). It is clear that tales of enchanted realms, of elves and dragons and questing heroes, or of hauntings and other monstrous intrusions of the supernatural into our workaday world, are favoured by many millions of readers. In the present volume I attempt to define the category by describing a hundred notable novels which seem to me to be fantasies of one sort or another. All were written in English, and all first appeared in book form between 1946 and 1987.

Of course, the terms 'fantasy' and 'the fantastic' are open to dozens of interpretations, and I shall not try to choose between theoretical definitions here. An academic commentator, Rosemary Jackson, has complained: 'As a critical term, "fantasy" has been applied rather indiscriminately to any literature which does not give priority to realistic representation: myths, legends, folk and fairy tales, utopian allegories, dream visions, surrealist texts, science fiction, horror stories . . .' But it seems to me that fantasy *is* an indiscriminate form, one wholly without good manners and literary decorum. Insofar as it constitutes a genre, fantasy is a capacious hold-all of the supernatural and the uncanny, the visionary and the repellent. We may even view it as a primal genre, essentially formless, a swamp which has served as the breeding ground for all other popular fictional genres (they arise, they enjoy their flourishing moments in the sun, then they gradually sink back into the swamp – where in time their dead parts will nourish other genres). So in lieu of a rigorous definition, here is a thumbnail history of the fantastic in fiction.

It has been remarked often enough that fantasy is at least as old as literature. Up to the eighteenth century, almost all narrative fictions, both verse and prose, were fantastic to a greater or lesser degree. In the first half of the eighteenth century a new form of prose fiction arose, aptly named the Novel. Unlike the epics and satires, the chivalric romances and other 'mouldy tales' which had preceded it, the novel was predominantly a realistic form: it dealt with day-to-day life in a matter-of-fact way, concerning itself in the main with love, money, class, social niceties and the comedy of manners. The realistic novel had a revolutionary impact on English writing (and, later, on world writing); befitting an age of science and reason, it became (and remains) the dominant form, the touchstone of modern literature. However, the impulse to fantasy remained, and the fantastic soon reasserted itself in English fiction. It did so in the form of the first significant sub-genre of the modern novel, namely the Gothic Tale of Terror. The earliest fantasy novels – that is to say, the earliest works which were both novels *and* fantasies – were those late eighteenth and early nineteenth-century books by Horace Walpole, Clara Reeve, William Beckford, Anne Radcliffe, M. G. Lewis, Mary Shelley and Charles Maturin which we now regard as the classics of the Gothic movement. For roughly fifty years, from *The Castle of Otranto* in 1764 to *Melmoth the Wanderer* in 1820, the Gothic romance was the most popular kind of fiction, displacing the realistic novel (as practised by, say, Fanny Burney and Jane Austen) in the affections of a majority of readers.

The appeal of realism proved enormously strong, however, and as the nineteenth century wore on the realistic novel became ever more deeply entrenched as the leading form of fiction. This was the age of the great novelists: the Brontës, Thackeray, Dickens, Trollope, George Eliot. Fantasy never quite died, but it was driven more and more into 'lowly', popular forms which were sub-categories of the novel proper – fiction for children, penny dreadfuls, yellowback sensation novels, and so on. As the day of the Gothic romance waned, new sub-genres arose, all of them in a sense offspring of the Gothic tale of terror: the historical novel, the romantic love story, the crime thriller, the imperial tale of adventure. In these genres, ancestors of so many of today's publishing categories, the fantastic elements were reduced to a minimum: these were pseudo-realistic fictions, with heightened colour, atmosphere and melodrama. By the time of Thomas Hardy and Henry James the 'serious' realistic novel stood supreme, with the pseudo-realism of the popular genres to buttress it. But no sooner had this balance been achieved than fantasy began to make a surprising return: it crept out of the nursery, the dime novels and the yellowbacks and into the middlebrow magazines and bestselling hardcovers. George MacDonald and William Morris wrote magical romances; Bram Stoker wrote *Dracula*. The English ghost story flourished at the beginning of the twentieth century, and so did the scientific romance of H. G. Wells and his imitators (an entirely new form of 'realistic fantasy' which of course led to the modern genre of science fiction). After the turn of the century a new tradition of otherworldly fantasy was gradually established by writers such as Lord Dunsany, E. R. Eddison, David Lindsay and – in America – by James Branch Cabell, A. Merritt, H. P. Lovecraft and Clark Ashton Smith (although most of them worked obscurely). In serious literature, realism remained the norm, even if it was challenged by a Modernism which occasionally tended towards the fantastic. But a countertradition now existed, a fairly large body of 'adult fantasy' which is immediately ancestral to most of the post-1945 fantastic fiction that I describe in this book.

So much for the prehistory. Fantasy may be an ancient fictional form, but in another sense it is one of the youngest of commercial genres. As a publishers' category it is actually younger than its own technocratic offspring, science fiction. And as a category it belongs more to America than to Britain. There were various harbingers, but the great American publishing boom in fantasy really got under way in the mid to late 1960s (sf had enjoyed its initial boom a dozen years earlier). The books that first defined the category were the rival US paperback editions of J. R. R. Tolkien's *The Lord of the Rings* (*16*), which appeared in 1965–6. Simultaneously, Robert E. Howard's 'Conan' books (*8*) were re-edited by L. Sprague de Camp for a successful paperback series. Hundreds of thousands of Tolkien's and Howard's books were sold to a largely young audience which apparently wished to turn its back on a scientific and technological world. These twin influences – the British tradition of genteel fantasy sprung from nursery tales; and the American tradition of fantastic adventure fiction sprung from the pulp magazines – were swiftly reinforced by the work of several other writers who happened to be well placed at the right time. Ira Levin's *Rosemary's Baby* (*35*), the first modern supernatural-horror novel to achieve best-selling status, appeared in 1967. Fritz Leiber's sword-and-sorcery tales of 'Fafhrd and the Gray Mouser' (*40*) were re-edited and published in paperback for the first time from 1968. Michael Moorcock's 'Elric' and 'Hawkmoon' epics began to appear in the US in 1967 (*30*). Two highly influential works appeared in 1968 – Ursula Le Guin's *A Wizard of Earthsea* (*39*) and Peter Beagle's *The Last Unicorn* (*38*). Between them, these books were responsible for launching modern fantasy as a successful commercial genre. Tolkien apart, the leading novels of the 1970s –

especially the works of Stephen King and Stephen R. Donaldson – were to achieve greater sales, but it was the group of books which appeared in the late 1960s that began the upward soar in fantasy's fortunes.

However, for several good reasons, I have chosen to date my list of the hundred 'best' modern fantasy novels from the late 1940s rather than the late 1960s. One reason is that this allows me to begin with Mervyn Peake's *Titus Groan*, a favourite novel of mine (and, moreover, one which did not enjoy any general popularity until twenty-odd years after its first publication). Apart from Peake, many writers who were to become important in the modern fantasy field began their careers in the 1940s: L. Sprague de Camp, Fritz Leiber, Jack Vance and Poul Anderson, to name but four. It was also the decade in which J. R. R. Tolkien wrote his massively influential *The Lord of the Rings* – eventually published in 1954. Fantasy may not have been very visible during the forties and fifties, but significant works were beginning to appear and an audience's tastes were being formed. Another reason I chose to begin in the post-war period is that I conceived this volume as a companion to my earlier book, *Science Fiction: The 100 Best Novels* (Xanadu Publications, 1985). That work covered the years 1949 to 1984, and, with a little stretching at both ends, this one covers much the same period. Nevertheless, my selection of a hundred titles is heavily weighted towards the sixties, seventies and eighties, and this is because the genre has enjoyed its greatest growth during the past two-and-a-half decades. If 1953 was something of a peak year for science fiction (see the listing in my previous book), then 1984 would seem to be a similar high point for modern fantasy. Or perhaps it is too soon to tell. We are still living in the boom years of fantasy fiction; nor is any end in sight.

Literary critics may disapprove of fantasy for various reasons, and in my view one of the most potent is the commonly expressed argument that fantasy is a literature of *reaction*. Thus, the Austrian critic Franz Rottensteiner:

'modern fantasy is a reaction to industrial society and its pressures . . . It is not chance that this kind of fantasy arose in nineteenth-century England, the country that first felt the full pressure of industrialization; that its main practitioners, whether Morris, Lord Dunsany, C. S. Lewis, E. R. Eddison, or J. R. R. Tolkien, all profoundly disliked their own time; or that this literature reached its greatest popularity in the scientifically and industrially most advanced country on Earth (the US), and then spread from there to other countries. Modern fantasy is a literature for a discontented city population . . .' (*S-F Studies* No. 23, March 1981). I believe this to be largely true, and it is the uneasiness this thought provokes which causes me marginally to prefer science fiction to fantasy – although it must be acknowledged that a simple-minded reaction against science and technology does not necessarily characterize *all* modern fantasy. As may become clear from my comments on particular works, I favour the types of fantasy which do engage in some way with the real world. I am as susceptible to the lure of romantic escapism as most readers, but in the end I cannot help feeling that any really good novel should tell me some truth about life. Indeed, the best fantasies do this in innumerable ways – some by straightforward allegory, others by a more arcane symbolism, some by wit and subtlety of characterization, and many by the seemingly authentic manner in which they project the archetypal hopes and fears, the moods and shadings, of the human mind. (The 'truest' fantasies present us with an inner landscape, one might almost say a spiritual landscape, which may well have psychological and mythological depths.) All imaginative writing, even that in which the subject-matter seems centuries removed, does reflect its period of composition. Whatever their trappings, these fantasy novels are inevitably the fantasies of our age; they speak to the second half of the twentieth century.

As I pointed out in my introduction to *SF: The 100 Best*, modern fantastic fiction tends to fall into two broad divisions, the Supernatural Horror story and the Heroic Fantasy: 'By the supernatural horror story I mean such works as Stoker's *Dracula*, the stories of H. P. Lovecraft and most of the books of Stephen King. Characteristically, these describe the irruption of some supernatural force into the everyday world, and they are horrific precisely because the forces and phenomena described are irrational – which is to say they are inexplicable in terms of the scientific world view. By heroic fantasy I mean such works as Tolkien's *The Lord of the Rings*, the whole sword-and-sorcery sub-genre, and all those books which carry titles like *The Elfstones of Shannara*. Usually, these are set in completely imaginary worlds, never-never lands where the modern scientific world view is suspended and "magic" rules. The emotional tenor of these works is not so much horrific as pleasurably escapist.' Many of my chosen hundred fit into one or the other of these major branches of fantasy. But on reflection I believe a third division should be added: an approximate grouping which one may call the Fabulation, or absurdist metafiction – stories which are set in the real world, but which distort that world in ways other than the supernaturally horrific. Several of the finest novels described here fall into this last category: the books by Thomas Pynchon, Angela Carter, John Crowley and Geoff Ryman, for instance.

So the scope of my selection is broad. Yet, as was the case with my book on science fiction, I must offer apologies here for numerous omissions. There are no foreign-language fantasies represented, for I feel they would have made my book unwieldy (all those Latin American 'magic realists'!). I have included some children's fantasies, particularly those which have been enjoyed by adult readers, but not a great many of them – on the basis that most children's fiction is fantasy, and if I were to stray too far in that direction I would not know where to stop. Hence the omission of such worthy writers as Madeleine L'Engle, Susan Cooper, William Mayne, Lloyd Alexander, Russell Hoban, Diana Wynne-Jones, Robin McKinley and Roald Dahl, among many others. Again, I have included a certain amount of 'light' fantasy, but not a great deal of it – so apologies to the fans of Piers Anthony, Robert Asprin, Jack L. Chalker, Terry Pratchett, Mike Resnick and others among that growing band of entertainers. I have found room for some mighty tomes (Stephen R. Donaldson, Guy Gavriel Kay), but perhaps I should have included yet more trilogies and multi-volume series – the works of Evangeline Walton, Louise Cooper, Barbara Hambly, Katherine Kurtz, David Eddings, Tanith Lee, Paul Hazel, Nancy Springer, Cherry Wilder, Judith Tarr and Raymond E. Feist are a few that come to mind: in some cases I was daunted by the sheer size of these *oeuvres* and in others I was unimpressed by their essentially repetitive, formulaic nature. As before, I admit to blind spots and to ignorance. This is no infallible selection, merely a guide to some good reading in a fantastic vein. I have tried to make a balanced list, and in doing so I have included some books which are not really to my taste – they may well be other people's favourites, though. In truth there are not a hundred masterpieces of modern fantasy, any more than there are a hundred masterpieces of science fiction.

But how do my choices compare with other readers' preferences? The August 1987 issue of the American sf/fantasy news magazine *Locus* contained an interesting list of 'All-Time Best Fantasy Novels', as decided in a postal ballot of the magazine's readership. My list of a hundred novels was largely determined by the time these poll results appeared, but I give the *Locus* 'top thirty-three' here as a comparison (the titles are ranked in descending order of popularity):

1 *The Lord of the Rings* by J. R. R. Tolkien (1954–55)

2 *The Hobbit* by J. R. R. Tolkien (1937)

3 *A Wizard of Earthsea* by Ursula Le Guin (1968)

4 *The Shadow of the Torturer* by Gene Wolfe (1980)

5 *The Last Unicorn* by Peter S. Beagle (1968)

6 *The Once and Future King* by T. H. White (1958)

7 *Nine Princes in Amber* by Roger Zelazny (1970)

8 *The Chronicles of Thomas Covenant* by Stephen R. Donaldson (1977)

9 *Dragonflight* by Anne McCaffrey (1968)

10 *Little, Big* by John Crowley (1981)

11 *Alice in Wonderland* by Lewis Carroll (1865)

12 *The Gormenghast* trilogy by Mervyn Peake (1946–59)

13 *The Riddlemaster of Hed* by Patricia A. McKillip (1976)

14 *The Incomplete Enchanter* by L. Sprague de Camp and Fletcher Pratt (1941)

15 *Watership Down* by Richard Adams (1972)

16 *The Dying Earth* by Jack Vance (1950)

17 *Glory Road* by Robert A. Heinlein (1963)

18 *A Spell for Chameleon* by Piers Anthony (1977)

19 *Dracula* by Bram Stoker (1897)

20 *The Wizard of Oz* by L. Frank Baum (1900)

21 *Silverlock* by John Myers Myers (1949)

22 *Something Wicked This Way Comes* by Ray Bradbury (1962)

23 *The White Dragon* by Anne McCaffrey (1978) / *The Stand* by Stephen King (1978)

25 *Lord Valentine's Castle* by Robert Silverberg (1980)

26 *The Chronicles of Narnia* by C. S. Lewis (1950–56)

27 *The Shining* by Stephen King (1977)

28 *Conjure Wife* by Fritz Leiber (1953)

29 *Deryni Rising* by Katherine Kurtz (1970) / *The Worm Ouroboros* by E. R. Eddison (1922)

31 *Witch World* by Andre Norton (1963)

32 *'Salem's Lot* by Stephen King (1975)

33 *A Wrinkle in Time* by Madeleine L'Engle (1962)

Some of these titles (*Alice in Wonderland, Dracula,* etc.) were published well before my chosen period, which begins in 1946. Others are arguably science fiction rather than fantasy proper (for example, the Anne McCaffrey and Robert Silverberg books, which are set on alien planets). Of the remainder, the great majority do appear in my hundred.

In the last couple of decades, various awards have been established for fantasy fiction. The World Fantasy Awards, familiarly known as the 'Howards', were created in 1975 (in imitation of the Hugo Awards for science fiction, which have been established since the 1950s). These awards are determined by a panel of critics, and are presented at the World Fantasy Convention which is held in October every year (usually in the United States). The winners in the category of best novel have been as follows:

For 1974 *The Forgotten Beasts of Eld* by Patricia A. McKillip

For 1975 *Bid Time Return* by Richard Matheson

For 1976 *Doctor Rat* by William Kotzwinkle

For 1977 *Our Lady of Darkness* by Fritz Leiber

For 1978 *Gloriana* by Michael Moorcock

For 1979 *Watchtower* by Elizabeth A. Lynn

For 1980 *The Shadow of the Torturer* by Gene Wolfe

For 1981 *Little, Big* by John Crowley

For 1982 *Nifft the Lean* by Michael Shea

For 1983 *The Dragon Waiting* by John M. Ford

For 1984 { *Mythago Wood* by Robert Holdstock / *Bridge of Birds* by Barry Hughart

For 1985 *Song of Kali* by Dan Simmons

For 1986 *Perfume* by Patrick Suskind

About half of the above titles are included in my list. There is also a lesser-known British Fantasy Award (officially called the August Derleth Fantasy Award) which has been in existence for slightly longer. Perhaps it reflects popular taste more accurately than the World Fantasy Award, since the winners are determined by the entire membership of each year's British Fantasy Convention (usually held in the summer) rather than by a panel of experts. The winning titles in the novel category have been:

For 1971 *The Knight of the Swords* by Michael Moorcock

For 1972 *The King of the Swords* by Michael Moorcock

For 1973 *Hrolf Kraki's Saga* by Poul Anderson

For 1974 *The Sword and the Stallion* by Michael Moorcock

For 1975 *The Hollow Lands* by Michael Moorcock

For 1976 *The Dragon and the George* by Gordon R. Dickson

For 1977 *A Spell for Chameleon* by Piers Anthony

For 1978 *The Chronicles of Thomas Covenant* by Stephen R. Donaldson

For 1979 *Death's Master* by Tanith Lee

For 1980 *To Wake the Dead* by Ramsey Campbell

For 1981 *Cujo* by Stephen King

For 1982 *The Sword of the Lictor* by Gene Wolfe

For 1983 *Floating Dragon* by Peter Straub

For 1984 *Incarnate* by Ramsey Campbell

For 1985 *The Ceremonies* by T. E. D. Klein

For 1986 *It* by Stephen King

Rather fewer of these titles have made their way on to my list – but then there does seem to have been a heavy emphasis on horror fiction in the more recent British Fantasy Awards, and although I have certainly not avoided supernatural horror novels I have represented them sparingly in the selection of one hundred books which follows. Horror is a category which straddles genres: some of it is fantasy, some is science fiction, and some of it is purely 'psychological' (Robert Bloch's *Psycho* is the paradigm of the modern non-fantasy horror novel). I can commend Steven Jones's and Kim Newman's forthcoming 'rival' volume, *Horror: The 100 Best Books* (Xanadu, 1988), as an authoritative guide to the latter-day tale of terror.

So now we come to my hundred. 'If you disagree violently with some of my choices I shall be pleased. We arrive at values only through dialectic.' Thus Anthony Burgess in his book *Ninety-Nine Novels: The Best in English Since 1939*. The following list of 'the best' invites similar disagreement, yet I remain confident that at least some of the novels I have selected are masterpieces of modern literature, full of beauty and wonder. The others are craftsmanlike entertainments which I happily commend to you for your enjoyment.

David Pringle
Brighton, January 1988

BRIEF BIBLIOGRAPHY

Although at least two encyclopedias of fantasy fiction have been promised for some years, I have yet to see one. Meanwhile, *The Encyclopedia of Science Fiction* edited by Peter Nicholls and John Clute (London: Granada, and New York: Doubleday, 1979) remains a very useful, if rapidly dating, reference work. Most of the authors dealt with here have entries in the Nicholls/Clute encyclopedia, even though some of them have written no science fiction. Another reference book of note is *Who's Who in Horror and Fantasy* by Mike Ashley (London: Elm Tree, 1977).

General critical surveys of the fantasy field which I have found valuable include *Imaginary Worlds: The Art of Fantasy* by Lin Carter (New York: Ballantine, 1973) and *The Fantasy Book: An Illustrated History from Dracula to Tolkien* by Franz Rottensteiner (London: Thames & Hudson, 1978). An informal, chatty, but continually interesting exploration of the horror fantasy field (mainly movies) is *Stephen King's Danse Macabre* (London: Macdonald, 1981). Michael Moorcock's *Wizardry and Wild Romance: A Study of Epic Fantasy* (London: Gollancz, 1987) appeared when my book was almost complete, but I was already familiar with sections of it which had appeared elsewhere – particularly the amusing chapter called 'Epic Pooh' which was first published as a chapbook in 1976.

The more rigorously theoretical and academic works on the subject include *Modern Fantasy: Five Studies* by C. N. Manlove (Cambridge University Press, 1975), *The Game of the Impossible: A Rhetoric of Fantasy* by W. R. Irwin (Urbana,

Illinois, 1976), *Fantasy: The Literature of Subversion* by Rosemary Jackson (London: Methuen, 1981) and *The Impulse of Fantasy Literature* by C. N. Manlove (London: Macmillan, 1983).

Biographical studies which have proved useful to me are *Mervyn Peake* by John Watney (London: Michael Joseph, 1976), *J. R. R. Tolkien: A Biography* by Humphrey Carpenter (London: Allen & Unwin, 1977) and *The Inklings: C. S. Lewis, J. R. R. Tolkien, Charles Williams, and their Friends* by Humphrey Carpenter (London: Allen & Unwin, 1978). Also invaluable for general reference is Carpenter's *The Oxford Companion to Children's Literature* (written in collaboration with Mari Prichard; Oxford University Press, 1984).

I have been influenced by much that has appeared in *Foundation: The Review of Science Fiction*, which I edited from 1980 to 1986. (The present editor is Edward James, c/o The SF Foundation, North East London Polytechnic, Longbridge Road, Dagenham, RM8 2AS). I must also pay tribute to *Locus: The Newspaper of the Science Fiction Field*, edited by Charles N. Brown (PO Box 13305, Oakland, CA 94661, USA), and to the now defunct *Fantasy Review*, edited by Robert A. Collins.

1

MERVYN PEAKE

Titus Groan

This is one of the greatest fantasy novels in the language. Frequently described as 'Gothic', *Titus Groan* contains no obvious supernatural elements. Yet it is unutterably strange, a tragicomedy of fantastic dimensions. The story unfolds in a vast, decaying castle known as Gormenghast, which seems to stand in a parallel world somewhere outside our own space and time. The names of the characters are English (Dickensian English) but the setting is not England. Gormenghast exists in some allegorical domain, a stony world of ancient rituals and ossified traditions, which may, just possibly, be symbolic of a declining Britain (or a declining European civilization). But the book does not have an allegorical feel: despite their ludicrous or portentous names – Rottcodd, Mr Flay, Swelter, Dr Prunesquallor, Sourdust, Nanny Slagg – the characters seem real; we become involved in their fates; they are not mere 'humours'.

The long, slow narrative is chiefly concerned with the birth and early childhood of Titus, heir to Lord Sepulchrave, the 76th Earl of Groan – and with the rebellion of Steerpike, a bulging-browed, cold-eyed kitchen boy who apparently wishes to rise in the world by pulling the castle down around his ears. In one of the first great set-pieces of the novel, Steerpike climbs to the castle's rooftops: 'faint and dizzy with fatigue and emptiness and with the heat of the strengthening sun, he saw spread out before him in mountainous façades a crumbling panorama, a roofscape of Gormenghast, its crags and its stark walls of cliff pocked with nameless windows.' Steerpike realizes that he cannot pit himself against this forbidding architecture, but that he can work *within* it: he can discover all its secret rooms and corridors, and learn the wily arts of ingratiation and manipulation. So he follows this course, befriending Titus's teenage sister Fuchsia and her feeble-minded aunts, Cora and Clarice Groan, among others. Eventually he burns Lord Sepulchrave's library, repository of all Gormenghast's lore and ritual, and thereby drives the old Earl to madness and death. There is also a titanic battle between the cadaverous Mr Flay, Lord Sepulchrave's servant, and the castle's monstrous cook, Swelter, which results in the banishment of one and the death of the other. But the ancient order is partially restored, and the novel ends with the infant Titus inheriting his father's estate. 'His Infernal Slyness, the Archfluke Steerpike' remains at large, to continue his machinations in another volume (see the entry for Peake's *Gormenghast* [10]).

Mervyn Peake (1911–68), born in China of English parents, was first and foremost a visual artist. Trained as a painter and illustrator, he turned to writing during World War II (much of *Titus Groan* was written while he was serving as a gunner and a bomb-disposal expert in the British army). He proved to be a brilliant artist in prose. Not surprisingly, one of his chief strengths lies in the vivid description of imaginary architectures and landscapes. Yet, as I have said, his people are also amazingly real – Steerpike, in particular, is a remarkable creation: twisted, spiteful, but heroic withal. And the plot in which Peake's characters are all enmeshed is both comical and terrifying. Once experienced, the world and the characters of *Titus Groan* cannot be forgotten.

First edition: London, Eyre & Spottiswoode, 1946 (hardcover)
First American edition: New York, Reynal & Hitchcock, 1946 (hardcover)
Most recent edition: London, Methuen (paperback)

2

A. E. VAN VOGT

The Book of Ptath

From the sublime to the ridiculous. Unlike Mervyn Peake, Alfred Elton van Vogt (born 1912) is the quintessential pulp-fiction writer. His wildly extravagant stories appealed to the wartime readers of John W. Campbell's influential magazines *Astounding Science Fiction* and *Unknown Worlds*, where he was for some years the most popular contributor. Van Vogt's 'nearly invincible alien beasts, the long time-spans of his tales, the time paradoxes they were filled with, the quasi-messianic supermen who came into their own as their stories progressed, the empires they tended to rule, all were presented in a prose that used crude, dark colours but whose striking sense of wonder was conveyed with a dreamlike conviction. The complications of plot for which he became so well known, and which have been so scathingly mocked for their illogic and preposterousness . . . are best analysed, and their effects best understood, when their sudden shifts of perspective and rationale and scale are seen as analogous to the movements of a dream' – according to the admirable critic John Clute, in *The Encyclopedia of Science Fiction*.

The Book of Ptath was first published in shorter form in 1943, in the very last issue of *Unknown Worlds*. (The magazine is supposed to have died as a result of the paper shortage, but its sister magazine carried on, and a more likely explanation for *Unknown*'s demise after a mere four years of publication is that pulp fantasy simply did not have the mass popularity of science fiction in those days.) The story, very much about a 'quasi-messianic' superman coming into his own, is set some two hundred million years in the future – in a land called Gonwonlane (the ancient super-continent of Gondwanaland, now reformed). The hero, Ptath, can remember nothing but his own name. He has enormous strength and great powers of recuperation, and he feels a compulsion to travel towards a distant city, also named Ptath. This he begins to do, swatting aside patrolling soldiers and anyone else who tries to hinder him. In the city, a beautiful but evil woman called Ineznia awaits him. She is a goddess, and Ptath is a reincarnated god (no less): she has recalled him to life in order to undergo a series of challenges which will end in his destruction for all time . . .

Along the way, Ptath recalls one of his previous identities: he is Peter Holroyd, an American tank-corps captain from World War II. He has been plucked from an unimaginably remote past to take part in this battle of titans in an equally unthinkable future. Not surprisingly, he remains in a state of mental confusion throughout most of the novel – as does the reader, for the plot is speedy and complex, strewn with revelations and reversals, characters who inhabit others' bodies, apparently arbitrary feats of magic, dread secrets revealed in almost every chapter. Eventually Ptath is reunited with his beloved L'onee (who has been held captive by the wicked goddess), discovers his destiny, and breaks Ineznia's power. For any reader who is willing to lapse into the correct frame of mind, it is all highly enjoyable. A. E. van Vogt is a graceless but energetic writer, and his story carries its own lunatic sense of conviction.

First edition: Reading, Pennsylvania, Fantasy Press, 1947, (hardcover)
First British edition: London, Sidgwick & Jackson, 1967 (in *A Van Vogt Omnibus*, hardcover)
Most recent edition: London, Granada (paperback)

3

FLETCHER PRATT

The Well of the Unicorn

Two of the early twentieth-century masters of fantasy fiction were the Irishman Lord Dunsany, author of *The King of Elfland's Daughter* (1924) and many other tales, and the Yorkshireman E. R. Eddison, best remembered for his epic novel *The Worm Ouroboros* (1922). The works of Dunsany and Eddison fall outside the scope of this book, but it is worth noting here that their influence lives on in much post-World War II fantasy – including this striking novel by the American writer Fletcher Pratt (1897–1956). In fact, *The Well of the Unicorn* is a sequel of sorts to Dunsany's two-act play 'King Argimenes and the Unknown Warrior' (written in 1910). Pratt pays tribute to 'a certain Irish chronicler', adding that 'the events he cites took place generations before any told here.'

This common world of Dunsany and Pratt is a pseudo-medieval never-never-realm full of evocative names: Dalarna, Acquileme, Salmonessa, Carrhoene, Vastmanstad, Uravedu and the Spice Islands. Pratt's young hero is called Airar Alvarson, and his adventures are set in motion when he is robbed of his inheritance by the cruel Vulking overlords. Cast out of his ancestral home and forced to survive on his wits, Airar soon encounters a wizard named Meliboë, who gives him an enchanted ring . . . This is the stuff of fairy-tale, though recounted in a dryly humorous and peculiarly knotty prose style – as in this passage where Airar, himself a fledgling sorcerer, has been asked to cast a protective spell over an old ship which belongs to his allies the Free-fishers:

. . . Airar must take his book forthwith down to the iulia and make what could be made. He got them all out of the hold with some difficulty (for they were curious and pleaded Doctor Meliboë had never used them so), and set up his pentacle on the roundstone where the fire had been, night agone. As soon as the first words of power were repeated Airar could feel how the whole ship stank of old magics, stronger and more deadly than any he knew. They tore at his throat and entrails as though he had swallowed a new-born dragon-pup . . .

He lifted the spell to the second stage then and they came all around him, yammering horribly just beyond the protective figure, with faces the utmost depths of evil that flavored like soft wax from form to form and always some feature disgustingly bloated or misplaced, promising or threatening to make him cease his runes. The pentacle held tight, but it wrung him through to hear those voices with their high-pitched note like a knife on marblestone that the mind could hardly bear, and when he came to the sobrathim-spell it was all he could do to keep from the yell of anguish that would give them power and him death. Somehow he managed; could feel the protection settling round him and ship in a heavy grey opaque curtain, almost physically visible, with the displaced powers piping and muttering angrily out in the glooms beyond.

Airar is caught up in a rebellion against the Vulkings; he travels, fights, falls in love with the seemingly unattainable Princess Argyra, and learns much of the ways of the world. Interspersed throughout are tales of the fabled unicorn's well, that ever-fleeting mirage of peace. *The Well of the Unicorn* is a long and complex novel, predominantly realistic in tone despite its fantastic setting. It may be a work of 'swordplay and sorcery', but (in the words of Pratt's erstwhile collaborator L. Sprague de Camp) it is also 'an appealing love story and a shrewd and subtle commentary on problems of politics, morals and philosophy.'

First edition: New York, Sloane, 1948 (hardcover)
Most recent edition: New York, Del Rey (paperback)

4

JACK WILLIAMSON

Darker Than You Think

'He rejoiced in the aroma of wet weeds and the redolence of decaying leaves. He liked even the cold dew that splashed his shaggy grey fur. Far from the too-loud clank and wheeze of the locomotive, he paused to listen to the tiny rustlings of field mice, and he caught a cricket with a flash of his lean forepaw . . . Elation lifted him: a clean, vibrant joy that he had never known. He raised his muzzle toward the setting half moon and uttered a quavering, long-drawn howl of pure delight . . .' Newspaperman Will Barbee is experiencing a weird but exhilarating dream – or is it reality? He is running free, a wolf in the night, all his senses alive as they never have been before. A white wolf bitch is calling out to him, and she seems to speak with the telepathic voice of a beautiful young woman (and fellow news-reporter) who calls herself April Bell. Will Barbee has known April for less than twenty-four hours, but already he is infatuated with her. They met at the local airport, where both had gone to cover the arrival of a famous anthropologist who was returning from the Gobi Desert with news of a momentous discovery. It had proved to be an abortive assignment, since the scientist dropped dead just as he was about to make his shattering announcement . . .

This is one of those novels that occupy the uncertain zone between science fiction and the supernatural horror story. It is about a hidden race of semi-human beings who are endowed with magical powers which enable them to change their forms by night, becoming wolves, tigers, snakes, whatever they will. These witch-folk have lived alongside normal humanity for many thousands of years, but now there is a real danger that their secret will be revealed to the world and they will all be hounded to death. The seductive April Bell recruits Barbee to their cause – for it turns out that he is a latent member of the witch-race, *Homo lycanthropus*. The distinguished anthropologist and his associates must die, before their findings from 'the pre-human burial mounds of Ala-shan' can be made public. Unfortunately, several of these people are good friends of Barbee's, and so he finds himself torn between his normal human loyalties and his new-found biological instincts. The story's sexual overtones are strong, and make the hero's internal struggle all the more convincing.

Jack Williamson (born 1908) uses a fair amount of pseudo-scientific patter, so it is possible for the reader to accept his modern treatment of the age-old werewolf theme as science fiction (Richard Matheson was to do something similar for the vampire theme in his novel *I am Legend*, 1954). Williamson is best known for his sf, which includes such slam-bang space-and-time operas of the 1930s as *The Legion of Space* and *The Legion of Time*. In contrast to those colourful mini-epics, *Darker Than You Think*, for all its excitements, is a relatively disciplined and thoughtful work. A shorter version first appeared in John W. Campbell's *Unknown* magazine in 1940. Expanded to book length in 1948, it now seems a little dated – but it still has a strong claim to being Williamson's best novel. The transformation scenes are vividly handled, and the unfolding of Barbee's strange predicament is engrossing right up to the unexpected (and rather wicked) denouement.

First edition: Reading, Pennsylvania, Fantasy Press, 1948 (hardcover)
First British edition: London, Sphere, 1976 (paperback)
Most recent edition: New York, Bluejay (paperback)

5

ROBERT GRAVES

Seven Days in New Crete

This intriguing book by a major English poet and historical
novelist is also well known under its American title, *Watch
the North Wind Rise*. At the time of its first appearance
Graves had just published his controversial non-fiction
work *The White Goddess: A Historical Grammar of Poetic
Myth* (1948), in which he argued that all great poetry is
inspired by the eternal feminine, the ancient triune Goddess
who has been displaced in modern times by male scientific
'reason'. *Seven Days in New Crete* deals with the same
subject-matter, in the form of a time-travel fantasy. The
narrator, a twentieth-century poet named Edward Venn-
Thomas, awakes in the far future to find himself in a
harmonious but dull utopia known as New Crete. It is a
wood-burning, candle-lit society run by poets and white
witches, where everyone expresses belief in the one true
Goddess. There is no violence – wars have become friendly
jousts fought on village greens – and there is surprisingly
little sexual activity ('in cases of complete sympathy we lie
side by side, or feet to feet, without bodily contact, and our
spirits float upward and drift in a waving motion around
the room').

Ostensibly, Edward Venn-Thomas has been invoked by
the witches in order to answer their questions about his
own period, the Late Christian Epoch. (His hosts' knowledge of the past is hazy: at one point he is galled to discover
one of his own poems in a book entitled *The English Poetic
Canon* – it has been 'clumsily re-written and attributed to
"the poet Tseliot"'.) But in fact, as he gradually comes to

realize, he is there to fulfil the Great Goddess's deeper designs. New Crete may be a non-violent paradise, but it is also boring and lifeless, and it is Edward's task to inject a little evil and insanity into the over-virtuous lives of its citizens. This he does, without at first being aware of what is happening: he becomes amorously involved with two young women, thus awakening feelings of jealousy which eventually lead to acts of murder and suicide. Edward says, in his major speech at the end of the novel:

'I am a barbarian, a poet from the past . . . I have a message to impart to you; listen well! The Goddess is omnipotent, the Goddess is all-wise, the Goddess is utterly good; yet there are times when she wears her mask of evil and deception. Too long, New Cretans, has she beamed on you with her gracious and naked face; custom and prosperity have blinded you to its beauty. In my barbarian epoch, a time of great darkness, she wore a perpetual mask of cruelty towards the countless rene-gades from her service, and lifted it, seldom and secretly, only for madmen, poets and lovers.

'. . . She summoned me from the past, a seed of trouble, to endow you with a harvest of trouble, since true love and wisdom spring only from calamity . . . Blow, North wind, blow! Blow away security; lift the ancient roofs from their beams; tear the rotten boughs from the alders, oaks and quinces; break down the gates . . . and set the madmen free . . .'

In this interesting (and often amusing) fantasy of conflict-ing impulses, Robert Graves (1895–1985) does not demand that we join him in his worship of the Goddess: rather, he explores all his own ambivalent feelings about poetry, womankind, technological progress, war and civilization.

First edition: New York, Creative Age Press, 1949
(hardcover, as *Watch the North Wind Rise*)
First British edition: London, Cassell, 1949 (hardcover)
Most recent edition: Oxford University Press (paperback)

6

JOHN MYERS MYERS

Silverlock

This curious item has long been popular in the United
States, though it is little known in Britain. In a recent poll
published by the sf/fantasy news magazine *Locus* (see p.
20), *Silverlock* was ranked twenty-first as 'All-Time Best
Fantasy Novel', just after L. Frank Baum's *The Wizard of
Oz* and ahead of such disparate works as C. S. Lewis's *The
Chronicles of Narnia* and Fritz Leiber's *Conjure Wife*. It is a
story of high adventure and fantastic transformations –
written throughout in a slangy, mid-twentieth-century
American style, a style redolent of cracker-barrels, Tall
Tales, and the tradition of so-called South-Western
humour. It also contains an underlying streak of brutality
which is not untypical of those rude influences. I suspect
that it owes something to the late nineteenth-century
American fantasist John Kendrick Bangs, author of *A
House-Boat on the Styx* (1896), a novel of the afterlife in
which numerous famous persons are gathered in humorous
juxtaposition.

Myers's hero and narrator, A. Clarence Shandon, is a
dislikeable young university graduate from the USA
('somewhere under the old hats, dry flies, and dead tennis
balls on the top shelf of a certain closet in Chicago you'll
find a sheepskin swearing that the U. of Wisconsin gave
me a degree in Business Administration'). At the opening
of the novel he is shipwrecked, and drifts for days before
being washed up, as exhausted as Odysseus at Nausicaa's
island or Gulliver in Lilliput, on the shore of a mysterious
land known simply as 'the Commonwealth'. It is not

inappropriate to evoke Odysseus and Gulliver, because Shandon soon finds that he has been stranded in a land of myths, legends, and famous fictional characters – although his response to all this is at first bone-headed and selfish. Soon after landing he meets a beautiful sorceress who turns him into a pig. He is rescued from Circe's swine-pen by a new-found friend, Golias, and together the pair go on to encounter Beowulf, Till Eulenspiegel, Manon Lescaut, Friar John, Anna Karenina, Prometheus, Don Quixote, Robin Hood, Raskolnikov, Sir Gawain and many others, with sundry cannibals, Vikings and Red Indians besides. The place-names of this unlikely Commonwealth include Watling Street, the House of Usher, Xanadu, Ilium and Utgard.

Shandon gains the nickname 'Silverlock', thanks to a characteristic streak of white hair, and as the tale progresses he matures, becoming less of a young boor and more of a perfect gentle knight. The narrative reaches its climax in the underworld, whither Shandon/Silverlock is led by a guide known as Faustopheles who at one point bids him to 'gaze into the Void and call it mother . . . You like to think that there's something so precious about you that the cosmos can't spare it. You know your body won't survive, but something tells you that your own private unit of life will be pickled in Time by the cherishing power that made it . . . This is your creator. Find love and warmth in it if you can, for in the end you're going back to it.' Silverlock emerges a wiser man from the nether regions, only to be carried away by the winged horse Pegasus and dumped once more in the ocean where all his adventures began.

John Myers Myers (born 1906) has produced a strange, harshly whimsical and rumbustious book, 'as live with incident as a beehive with buzz and as tirelessly busy' (in the words of one reviewer at the time of first publication). It will not be to every reader's taste, but it is memorably different.

First edition: New York, Dutton, 1949 (hardcover)
Most recent edition: New York, Ace (paperback)

7

L. SPRAGUE DE CAMP
AND FLETCHER PRATT

The Castle of Iron

We have already encountered Fletcher Pratt as the author of *The Well of the Unicorn* (*3*). In collaboration with Lyon Sprague de Camp (born 1907), he was also one of the most celebrated writers of what has been termed '*Unknown*-style fantasy'. The reference is to the late lamented pulp magazine in which many of these American authors first published their short stories and novellas – but it is a label which has come to signify more than just a common place and time of publication. *Unknown*-style fantasy was a new form of writing: modern in tone, light, snappy, and humorous. It tended to deal with supernatural events and characters in a 'rational' way. Mystical rhapsodies, crabbed lore, and deep dark dreads (of the sort made fashionable by H. P. Lovecraft and other *Weird Tales* authors of the 1930s) held little appeal for these writers.

The first collaborative book by de Camp and Pratt was *The Incomplete Enchanter* (1941). This delightful work, a conflation of two novellas, introduced the character of Harold Shea, a bold but accident-prone psychologist who plunges into one unlikely adventure after another. The anti-heroic Shea reappears in the sequel, *The Castle of Iron*, and in fact the two were later combined in one volume under the title *The Compleat Enchanter* (1975). It is pointless therefore to consider *The Castle of Iron* apart from its predecessor (all the material in the two books first appeared in *Unknown* during the early 1940s): we may as well treat them as one long episodic novel. At the beginning of the saga Harold Shea and his colleagues contrive a purely mental means of travelling to other worlds of possibility. Harold dubs this device the 'syllogismobile': by memorizing a complex set of formulae, he should be able to wish himself into the mythical realm of his choice.

But things invariably go awry. In his first outing, Harold, equipped with a Colt .38 and a copy of the *Boy Scout Handbook*, attempts to reach the world of ancient Irish myth. Instead he ends up in the land of the Norse sagas, where he encounters a grumpy Odin and a cruelly mischievous Loki, and becomes involved in the run-up to Ragnarok. Needless to say, his gun does not work and his handbook becomes instantly illegible. In his second trip, Harold is thrown into the world of Spenser's *Faerie Queene*; and in his third – the adventure narrated in the full-length novel *The Castle of Iron* – he finds himself in the fantastic realm of Ariosto's epic poem *Orlando Furioso* (compare Chelsea Quinn Yarbro's novel *Ariosto* [74]). Here he and his friends are trapped by sorcery in a castle built entirely of iron (in order to prevent it from rusting, its owners have to lubricate it regularly with foul-smelling olive oil). The humour is wry throughout, and the tone highly irreverent. Among many other far-fetched characters, Harold meets a Roland – the greatest of Charlemagne's twelve paladins – who has regressed to the mental age of three and now calls himself 'Snookums'. Luckily, Shea's psychological skills soon restore the hero's memory.

A later volume by de Camp and Pratt, *Wall of Serpents* (1960, also known as *The Enchanter Compleated*), contains two more Harold Shea adventures – this time set against the background of the Finnish *Kalevala* and old Celtic legends. These are also entertaining, though written at a less inspired pitch than that erudite and antic comedy *The Castle of Iron*.

First edition: New York, Gnome Press, 1950 (hardcover)
First British edition: London, Sphere, 1979 (paperback)
Most recent edition: New York, Ballantine (in *The Compleat Enchanter*, paperback)

8

ROBERT E. HOWARD

Conan the Conqueror

Conan, the mighty-thewed barbarian from the ancient land of Cimmeria, has become one of the myth figures of our time, portrayed on paperback book covers by the popular artist Frank Frazetta, in Marvel Comics titles (*The Savage Sword of Conan*, etc.) by numerous other artists, and, not least, on the cinema screen by the bodybuilder Arnold Schwarzenegger. Conan's success as a cultural icon is remarkable, rivalling that of Edgar Rice Burroughs's Tarzan of the Apes. It seems all the more remarkable when one considers that Conan's creator, a young Texan writer called Robert Ervin Howard (1906–36), died by his own hand some fourteen years before his first book was published. Howard wrote for *Weird Tales*, a grand old pulp magazine which specialized in supernatural horror stories (another of its luminaries was that other neurotic and short-lived American writer, Howard Phillips Lovecraft). It was in those shock-filled pages, in 1932, that Howard first presented Conan to the world. The hero battled his gory way through various short stories and novellas before starring in his first (and only) full-length yarn, 'The Hour of the Dragon' (serialized 1935–6). And it is this story which was republished in book form in 1950 as *Conan the Conqueror*.

It opens with a blood-curdling scene of necromancy: 'with a splintering crash, the carven lid of the sarcophagus burst outward as from some irresistible pressure applied from within, and the four men, bending eagerly forward, saw the occupant – a huddled, withered, wizened shape, with dried brown limbs like dead wood showing through

mouldering bandages . . . As they watched an awful transmutation became apparent. The withered shape in the
sarcophagus was expanding, was growing, lengthening.
The bandages burst and fell into brown dust. The shrivelled
limbs swelled . . .' The 3000-year-old sorcerer Xaltotun
has been brought back to life in order to help depose Conan
from the throne of Aquilonia. Conan, although a rude
northern barbarian and the son of a blacksmith, has succeeded in fighting his way to a kingship – and now jealous
forces are marshalling against him. Our hero is a formidable
man, described as 'mightily shouldered and deep of chest,
with a massive corded neck and heavily muscled limbs',
and he commands a huge army, so it is evident to his
enemies that only black magic can defeat him.

Xaltotun duly immobilizes Conan by sorcerous means,
defeats his army, and throws the deposed king into a
dungeon. A beautiful seraglio girl, Zenobia, helps Conan
escape ('I have loved you, King Conan, ever since I saw
you riding at the head of your knights'). He slays an
enormous ape which prowls the cells, then hacks his way
to freedom and begins the long task of winning back his
kingdom. Gradually he draws together his allies, learns his
enemies' weaknesses, and gains the magical assistance
which will enable him to crush Xaltotun. Needless to say,
he succeeds – but the body-count is high. *Conan the
Conqueror* is a vigorous novel of bloody action, written in
true pulp-magazine style by a writer who has a flair for the
macabre. It is without intellectual distinction of any kind
(the names, for example, are poorly conceived – a rough-
hewn mixture drawn from Celtic, Greek and other miscel-
laneous sources), but it moves along well, and never fails
to deliver the crude excitements one might expect. This is
the original, unadulterated Sword-and-Sorcery, and as such
it has been extremely influential. Whatever his shortcom-
ings, Robert E. Howard managed to create a genre.

First edition: New York, Gnome Press, 1950 (hardcover)
First British edition: London, Boardman, 1954 (hardcover)
Most recent edition: New York, Ace, and London, Sphere
(paperbacks)

9

C. S. LEWIS

The Lion, the Witch
and the Wardrobe

According to Humphrey Carpenter's excellent book *The Inklings*, Professor J. R. R. Tolkien completed his great fantasy novel *The Lord of the Rings* (*16*) in 1949. Yet the first of its three volumes did not appear until 1954. During the five years that this masterpiece was making its slow way from the painstakingly revised manuscript to the finality of the printed page, Tolkien's good friend and fellow 'Inkling', Clive Staples Lewis (1898–1963), dashed off not one but *seven* highly successful fantasy novels for children. They are known collectively as 'The Chronicles of Narnia', since Narnia is the name of the magical land which is discovered by Lewis's young protagonists – a 'subcreation' analogous to Tolkien's Middle-earth. Carpenter tells us that Tolkien was not pleased, and disliked the first of these books, *The Lion, the Witch and the Wardrobe*, intensely: 'the story borrowed so indiscriminately from other mythologies and narratives (fauns, nymphs, Father Christmas, talking animals, anything that seemed useful for the plot) that for Tolkien the suspension of disbelief, the entering into a secondary world, was simply impossible. It just *wouldn't* "do", and he turned his back on it.' Yet Lewis's hastily-written stories have been loved by several generations of children and are frequently re-read by adults. They continue to sell copiously, and the first volume has been adapted as an animated film and a popular stage play. The other novels in the series are *Prince Caspian* (1951), *The Voyage of the 'Dawn Treader'* (1952), *The Horse and His Boy* (1953), *The Silver Chair* (1954), *The Magician's Nephew*

(1955) and *The Last Battle* (1956) – all of them completed by March 1953.

The children – Lucy, Susan, Peter and Edmund – enter the world of Narnia via an old wardrobe that stands in a disused room of the country house to which they have been evacuated during World War II. They find a wooded, snow-bound landscape peopled by fauns, dwarfs and various talking beasts. At present, Narnia is ruled by a wicked White Witch who has placed an enchantment on the land so that it is 'always winter, but it never gets to Christmas'. The weak-willed Edmund is won over to the Witch's cause by some inexpressibly delicious Turkish delight, but the other children side with the ordinary, suffering folk of their new-found land. Eventually they meet Narnia's champion of Good, the great tawny-maned lion called Aslan. The lion turns out to be a dying–god or Christ figure, who sacrifices himself in order to defeat the Witch and restore the natural order of the seasons to Narnia. Aslan is reborn, the wayward Edmund is redeemed, and all ends happily. The four children are restored to their own world, with the promise of many more adventures to come.

The novel is in part a Christian allegory, though Lewis does not rub his message in with too much force (many readers have later testified that they first read this story and its sequels with a simple pleasure in the unfolding fantasy, and no awareness of any 'hidden' content). The language is undemanding, and much of the invention whimsical. It is certainly a children's book, in the cosy tradition of Kenneth Grahame and A. A. Milne, but the death and resurrection of Aslan are genuinely moving, and the supernatural atmosphere – as expressed for instance in the chapter titles, 'Deep Magic from the Dawn of Time' and 'Deeper Magic from before the Dawn of Time' – is enough to send a pleasurable shiver down any young reader's spine.

First edition: London, Bles, 1950 (hardcover)
First American edition: New York, Macmillan, 1950 (hardcover)
Most recent editions: London, Fontana, and New York, Collier (paperbacks)

10

MERVYN PEAKE

Gormenghast

'Titus is seven. His confines, Gormenghast. Suckled on shadows; weaned, as it were, on webs of ritual: for his ears, echoes, for his eyes, a labyrinth of stone . . . He has learned an alphabet of arch and aisle: the language of dim stairs and moth-hung rafters. Great halls are his dim playgrounds: his fields are quadrangles: his trees are pillars.' Despite that ominous opening, the second of Peake's great novels about Titus Groan and his environs has a somewhat different flavour from the first. Titus himself is more to the fore, a vigorous, active child and youth – albeit that he bears the crushing weight of the 77th Earldom. In this book Gormenghast Castle seems livelier and more populous, and the outside world, the world of nature, impinges to a much greater degree.

We are introduced to the 'Professors' in their frightful common-room ('tobacco smoke had made of the place a kind of umber tomb'). These caricature English schoolmasters have names such as Fluke, Perch-Prism, Deadyawn, Cutflower and Bellgrove. The last-named is the most sympathetically portrayed, and the scenes in which he woos the ill-favoured Miss Irma Prunesquallor are very funny. It is the Professors' duty to teach the young Lord of Gormenghast, treating him as they would any other minor of the castle. As he endures their musty pedagogy, Titus dreams of the great outdoors, and eventually breaks away to play truant in the surrounding hills and forests (where he is befriended by the fearsome but loyal Mr Flay, who lurches like Frankenstein's monster through the trees, lamenting his long exile from the castle). Meanwhile the villainous kitchen-boy Steerpike has wormed his way into the service of Barquentine – the aged Master of Ritual, Keeper of the Observances, to whom he acts as 'Amanuensis'. Steerpike plans to murder Barquentine and assume his office – following which he will court Fuchsia, Titus's moody sister, and then perhaps kill the young Earl, thus becoming master of all he surveys.

As Steerpike's power waxes, Titus comes to loathe him. The story reaches an enthralling climax after a great deluge has flooded the castle, and Titus pursues Steerpike through the miles of drowned courtyards and corridors. As in Peake's *Titus Groan* (1) there are many wonderful 'painterly' descriptions along the way, both of the castle and of the surrounding countryside:

> . . . he was able to free his face of the leaves, and, as he panted to regain his breath, to see ahead of him, spreading into the clear distances, the forest floor like a sea of golden moss. From its heaving expanses, arose, as through the chimera of a daydream, a phantasmic gathering of ancient oaks. Like dappled gods they stood, each in his own preserve, the wide glades of moss flowing between them in swathes of gold and green and away into the clear, dwindling distances.
>
> When his breath came more easily, Titus realized the silence of the picture that hung there before him. Like a canvas of gold with its hundreds of majestic oaks, their winding branches dividing and sub-dividing into gilded fingertips – the solid acorns and the deep clusters of the legendary leaves.
>
> His heart beat loudly as the warm breath of the silence flowed about him and drew him in.

Perhaps *Gormenghast* is less of a unity than the earlier novel, but its finest moments, its revelations of character and landscape, are on a level with those in the first book. Both volumes are masterpieces of modern fantasy.

First edition: London, Eyre & Spottiswoode, 1950 (hardcover)
First American edition: New York, British Book Centre, 1950 (hardcover)
Most recent edition: London, Methuen (paperback)

11

JACK VANCE

The Dying Earth

Jack Vance (born 1920) was an unknown writer when this, his first book, was published obscurely in 1950. It is made up of six linked stories, none of which had appeared in magazines. Since then Vance has published dozens of stylish science fiction and fantasy novels, as well as several highly-praised crime thrillers (the latter under his full name of John Holbrook Vance). *The Dying Earth* is a remarkable work for a debut book, a classic of its type, and despite his later successes Vance has never quite surpassed it. The narratives are set in a mouldy, decaying but richly-coloured far-future world. We are in the twilight of the planet, and science has long since given way to magic. There are monsters in the shadows, plant-animal hybrids, vat-grown grotesques, and ghosts of millennia past. Against this haunted background we follow the antics of such characters as the would-be sorcerer Turjan of Miir and his enemy Mazirian the Magician. Although the plots of these tales are ingenious and amusing, much of their success is due to the evocation of atmosphere. Vance's prose is lyrical, and he has an eye for the colourful, as in this description of Mazirian's garden and its surroundings:

Certain plants swam with changing iridescences; others held up blooms pulsing like sea-anemones, purple, green, lilac, pink, yellow. Here grew trees like feather parasols, trees with transparent trunks threaded with red and yellow veins, trees with foliage like metal foil, each leaf a different metal – copper, silver, blue tantalum, bronze, green iridium. Here blooms like bubbles tugged gently upward from glazed green leaves, there a shrub bore a thousand pipe-shaped blossoms, each whistling softly to make music of the ancient Earth, of the ruby-red sunlight, water seeping through black soil, the languid winds. And beyond the roqual hedge the trees of the forest made a tall wall of mystery. In this waning hour of Earth's life no man could count himself familiar with the glens, the glades, the dells and deeps, the secluded clearings, the ruined pavilions, the sun-dappled plesaunces, the gullys and heights, the various brooks, freshets, ponds, the meadows, thickets, brakes and rocky outcrops.

The longest and last of the book's six tales concerns Guyal of Sfere, a young man who cannot cease from asking questions. He sets out to find the fabled Museum of Man, whose Curator may be able to answer all his queries. Along the way he acquires a beautiful girlfriend, and, with much trepidation, the two eventually set foot in the ruined Museum. Sure enough, they find a storehouse of forgotten lore and many fine artefacts of bygone times. 'What great minds lie in the dust,' muses Guyal. 'What gorgeous souls have vanished into the buried ages . . . Nevermore will there be the like; now, in the last fleeting moments, humanity festers rich as rotten fruit.' They find the aged Curator, close to death, and they help him defeat Blikdak, a vile demon which has grown from the mind of man. As the Curator explains: 'the sweaty condensation, the stench and vileness, the cloacal humours, the brutal delights, the rapes and sodomies, the scatophiliac whims, the manifold tittering lubricities that have drained through humanity formed a vast tumour; so Blikdak assumed his being.' They destroy the demon by ingenious means, the Curator dies, and Guyal assumes his place as the custodian of all knowledge. In the book's final scene the two young people gaze up at the white stars, asking themselves, 'what shall we do . . .?'

First edition: New York, Hillman, 1950 (paperback)
First British edition: London, Granada, 1972 (paperback)
Most recent editions: New York, Baen, and London, Grafton
(paperbacks)

12

SARBAN

The Sound of his Horn

This short tale of terror belongs to the great British tradition of creepy fireside yarns. The narrator, Alan Querdilion, tells his story to a pipe-smoking friend as they sit, late at night, before a hearth filled with crackling logs. But the wartime experiences which he recounts are far from cosy. 'Sarban' is the pseudonym of John W. Wall (born 1910), a writer known for his ghost stories. In an introduction written for the American edition, Kingsley Amis argues that *The Sound of his Horn*, although largely set in a meticulously imagined future, is fantasy rather than science fiction – 'the parallel universe in which the main story takes place is not to be approached by any kind of scientific technique'; moreover, the setting is rural (and neo-feudal), whereas the characteristic horrors of sf are usually urban.

Alan Querdilion tells of his escape from a German prison camp, and of his trek through the pine forests of Eastern Europe. In the bright moonlight, he comes across a fresh and enticing stretch of landscape: 'they were such different woods; not black, monotonous pine-forest, but a fair greenwood of oak and beech and ash and sweet white-flowering hawthorn.' He runs towards a small lake which is set amidst these trees, but stumbles into some magical energy-barrier and is struck unconscious: 'my eyes were pierced by a pain of yellow light, and my body, bereft of all its weight and cohesion, went whirling and spiralling upwards like a gas into the dark.' He awakes to find himself captive once more, in the hospital annexe of a luxurious hunting-lodge where he is tended by dumb servants. After

52

conversation with his doctor, he discovers that he has arrived in a future world where the Nazis have won World War II and where a vast stretch of Europe has been allowed to revert to primeval forest – a savage playground for its ruler, Count von Hackelnberg the Reich Master Forester.

Querdilion's narrative becomes nightmarish in the extreme. He hears the Count's hunting horn at night, 'sounded at long intervals, each [note] as lonely in the pitch dark and utter silence as one single sail on a wide sea'. He is permitted to watch a daylight hunt, and is horrified to find that the prey is not some unfortunate beast but an almost naked girl, her head and back bedecked with feathers like 'one of the bird-headed goddesses of Old Egypt.' Worse is to come: the Count not only pursues human prey, he also uses human 'hounds'. Pride of place in his ghastly menagerie is given to the cat-women – girls who have been 'sought and selected with connoisseur's care among all the slave-breeding farms of the Greater Reich . . . they were utterly unhuman: women transformed by a demonic skill in breeding and training into great, supple, swift and dangerous cats.' These ravening creatures are both beautiful and terrifying: Querdilion watches them tear apart two does with their claws and teeth. Then he is driven into the forest by the Count's men, himself to become the prey for the next hunt . . .

Sarban's slim novel is an expertly crafted horror piece, with compelling imagery and a very tense story-line. It undermines the sentimental notions, especially dear to English hearts, of the greenwood as a place of tranquillity, and of hunting as a sport of gentlemen. On one level, it is a straightforward tale of Nazi bestiality, if disturbing in its sexual implications. On another level, it is a timeless fantasy about human beings as hunters and hunted, about brutal humanity and brute nature.

First edition: London, Davies, 1952 (hardcover)
First American edition: New York, Ballantine, 1960 (paperback)
Most recent edition: London, Sphere (paperback)

13

FRITZ LEIBER

Conjure Wife

Fritz Leiber (born 1910) is a master of *modern* supernatural horror fiction. The traditional backcloths of Gothic horror tales – crumbling castles amidst dark woods, lonely mansions on windswept moors – are not for him. His stories are usually set in the cities and towns of contemporary America, and they concern bright up-to-the-minute people whose lives are shockingly disrupted by inexplicable terrors. Other writers have followed his example (they include such commercially successful authors as Ira Levin and Stephen King) but Leiber was there first, the pioneer. *Conjure Wife* was originally published in *Unknown Worlds* in 1943. The expanded text of the book version contains a number of references to atomic bombs and other post-1945 phenomena, but essentially it is the same tale as first horrified and delighted the wartime readers of John W. Campbell's magazine.

The plot concerns witchcraft in a university campus setting. Norman Saylor, a youngish professor of sociology, discovers that his wife, Tansy, has been performing 'Negro conjure magic' in secret. She collects nail-clippings, hair, horseshoe nails, even graveyard dirt – and uses these items, together with other potent detritus, to make charms which will ward off ill-luck and evil influences. Norman is a rational academic and the author of a book entitled *Parallelisms in Superstition and Neurosis*. He is appalled by this evidence of primitive behaviour in his own household and begs Tansy to abandon her childish nonsense. She puts up a spirited fight, but eventually gives in, and together they destroy all her magical paraphernalia. Immediately, things start to go badly wrong for Norman in his day-to-day work. A failed student threatens him with a gun, a girl accuses him of molesting her, and the college authorities begin to question minor irregularities in his private life . . .

Tansy reveals that she is not the only 'witch' on campus. For years she has been protecting her husband from the malicious attentions of other faculty members' wives. A coven of older women has been running local affairs, and now they intend to destroy Norman's career. They are attacking him in various ways – not least through his wife, who is now open to the malign effect of all their spells. When Tansy becomes hag-ridden by a demon which is intent on stealing her soul, Norman is forced to drop all his prejudices and learn the skills of that same 'conjure magic' which he once disdained. Only thus can he save his wife from being turned into a zombie – and simultaneously save his own job and academic reputation. Eventually he turns the tables on the university's monstrous matrons by a combination of arcane lore and modern academic know-how.

Conjure Wife is a frightening and at the same time amusing novel, based on the paranoid male's notion that *all* women are really witches. It has dated in certain obvious ways – one is much more aware nowadays of the sexism and racism implicit in the whole basis of the narrative – but nevertheless it remains a highly original, and seminal, tale of the supernatural. It may even have a strong appeal for female readers, since one can view the novel's central conceit as a quite deliberate attempt to undermine the whole business of masculine intellectual dominance: it adds up to a comic-horrific dream revenge by women on overweening male pride.

First edition: New York, Twayne, 1953 (hardcover)
First British edition: Harmondsworth, Penguin, 1969 (paperback)
Most recent edition: New York, Ace (paperback)

14

FRITZ LEIBER

The Sinful Ones

Like Leiber's *Conjure Wife*, *The Sinful Ones* first appeared in shorter magazine form. In this case, it may be that some readers are more familiar with the story under its original (and much more appropriate) title of 'You're All Alone' (*Fantastic Adventures* magazine, 1950). After Leiber expanded the novella for its 1953 paperback appearance, his publishers changed the title to *The Sinful Ones* and inserted a number of 'soft-porn' sex scenes – however, in a more recent edition [1980] those scenes have been rewritten to Leiber's latter-day taste. All this is unfortunate, but does not detract from the fact that *The Sinful Ones* (or 'You're All Alone') is one of the most original of modern horror fantasies.

The hero, Carr Mackay, has an unrewarding job in a Chicago employment agency. He also has a go-getting ladyfriend who continually exhorts him to better himself. Despite her blandishments, Carr is reluctant to join what seems to him to be a meaningless rat-race. One day, when he is feeling oddly alienated from his surroundings, a very frightened girl enters his office. She seems to be in flight from a large, menacing blonde woman whom Carr notices in the background. The girl fails to explain her own behaviour, but looks at Carr in fear and puzzlement, saying: 'Don't you really know what you are? Haven't you found out yet? . . . Maybe my bursting in here was what did it. Maybe I was the one who awakened you?' After she has scribbled him a note and left, Carr begins to learn what it means to be 'awake'. Still bewildered by the girl's sudden intrusion, he neglects his next client until he hears the man say, 'Thanks, I guess I will' and watches him pluck a non-existent cigarette out of the air and go through the motions of apparently lighting and smoking it. The client proceeds to hold a one-sided conversation, answering questions Carr has not uttered. It is as though the man is part of a huge clockwork mechanism, driven to do and say certain predictable things.

Carr soon discovers that almost everyone around him is behaving in this mechanical fashion. They are seemingly oblivious to him, ignoring his remarks, stepping around him, carrying on in a normal routine of existence which now seems risible in its predictability and lifelessness. It is as though Carr has suddenly fallen out of the clockwork machinery of urban life and gained a whole new existential freedom. He can move around the bustling city completely unseen, to all intents and purposes an invisible man. He can go anywhere at will and help himself to anything that he wants. But he will also suffer a terrible loneliness, unless he can make contact with other free spirits who are similarly 'awake'. The frightened girl, Jane, is one such, and luckily she has scribbled details of a rendezvous point on the piece of paper which she hurriedly passed to him. But why was she so terrified? And who was the menacing blonde lady? Are there hoodlums among Chicago's tiny population of 'invisible' persons – criminals who will make Carr's new life (and Jane's) a misery?

The Sinful Ones is an enjoyable thriller built on a simple but ingenious premise. Written at much the same time as David Riesman's best-selling sociological book *The Lonely Crowd*, but many years before the coinage of the phrases 'dropping out' and 'the counter-culture', it dramatizes a modern sense of urban alienation very effectively. It's a pity about those unnecessary sex scenes, though.

First edition: New York, Universal, 1953 (paperback)
Most recent edition: New York, Baen (paperback)

15

POUL ANDERSON

The Broken Sword

This full-blooded heroic fantasy about the Elfland of Old Norse legend was published at a time when fantasy novels of any type were rare commodities in the United States (although the 'Conan' books of Robert E. Howard were quietly issued by a small American press throughout the early 1950s). Anderson's novel remained out of print for a decade and a half before being revived (and revised) for the Ballantine Books 'Adult Fantasy' series in 1971. Despite its general neglect it has become an influential work, thanks to the enthusiasm of Michael Moorcock and a few other latter-day practitioners of Sword and Sorcery.

The Broken Sword is the tragic story of changeling half-brothers, the human-born Skafloc and the elf-born Valgard. Identical in appearance, and at first ignorant of each other's existence, they have very different natures: both are excellent warriors, though Skafloc is chivalrous and loving where Valgard is bloodthirsty and cruel. Skafloc, though human, gains all manner of skills from his elvish guardians: 'He learned the songs which could raise or lay storms, bring good or bad harvests, call forth either anger or peace in a mortal breast. He learned how to coax from their ores those metals, unknown to humans, which were alloyed in Faerie to take the place of steel. He learned the use of the cloak of darkness, and of the skins he could don to take the form of a beast. Near the end of his training he learned the mighty runes and songs and charms which could raise the dead, read the future, and compel the gods . . .'

Meanwhile the evil and un-human Valgard slays most of

his adoptive family, kidnaps his half-sister Freda, and flees from the lands of men. He takes service with Illrede the Troll-King, who has sworn to overthrow the rule of the elves in Faerie: 'Now for three days and nights Valgard's ships ran before an unchanging gale . . . He stood nearly the whole time in the prow of his craft, wrapped in a long leather cloak, salt and rime crusted on him, and brooded over the waters. Once a man dared gainsay him, and he slew the fellow on the spot and cast the body overboard. He himself spoke little, and that suited the crew, for they cared not to have that uncanny stare upon them.'

There is war between the elves and the trolls, a savage conflict in the realm of Faerie which remains invisible to human beings, and Skafloc and Valgard emerge as the champions of either side. Inevitably, they meet and fight, time and again. Their sister Freda becomes a prize in the battle. Skafloc falls in love with her, not realizing that she is kin to him, and she returns his love. Their sinful union leads to Skafloc's doom, though not before Valgard too has been destroyed. It is a grim, blood-soaked tale of parricide, fratricide and incest, frequently absurd and full of excess, but narrated with a lyrical fury which is astonishing in its emotional force. The prose is often purple with alliterations, but appropriately so: 'The wind skirled and bit at them. Sleet and spindrift blew off the waters in stinging sheets, white under the flying fitful moon. The sea bellowed inward from a wild horizon, bursting onto skerries and strand . . . The night was gale and sleet and surging waves, a racket that rang to the riven driven clouds.' This is a darkly magical story, as few modern fantasies are. Poul Anderson (born 1926) may have embroidered his material; nevertheless he remains true to the essential spirit of those Old Norse sagas which have inspired his remarkable novel.

First edition: New York, Abelard Schuman, 1954 (hardcover)
First British edition: London, Sphere, 1973 (paperback)
Most recent edition: New York, Del Rey (paperback)

16

J. R. R. TOLKIEN

The Lord of the Rings

As all the world knows, this massive work was first published in three volumes: *The Fellowship of the Ring*, *The Two Towers* and *The Return of the King*. Despite this, it is not so much a trilogy as one long, continuous novel. Over twelve years in the writing (it was mainly composed in the period from 1937 to 1949), and even longer in gestation (Tolkien first invented his 'Middle-earth' in the early 1920s), *The Lord of the Rings* is really the work of a lifetime. And it took another dozen years to gain wide acceptance: it was with the appearance of the second edition (1966), and with the nearly simultaneous publication of American paperback editions, that *The Lord of the Rings* finally took off and became one of the soaring best-sellers of twentieth-century fiction.

Why did it deserve its immense success? The first chapter, which describes the 'eleventy-first' birthday party of the hobbit Bilbo Baggins, is very juvenile in tone – and in fact it is a direct sequel to Tolkien's famous novel for young children, *The Hobbit, or There and Back Again* (1937). I must confess that for years I was unable to get beyond that opening chapter, with its little furry characters and cosy rural setting, its 'Bag End' and 'Hobbiton', and its tone so redolent of English nursery-tale humour. If I had been given this book to read when I was six years old I would probably have loved it – so I thought at the age of eighteen. But eventually I did read on; and I found myself succumbing to the spell, as millions of others have done before and since. As Bilbo's young kinsman, Frodo Baggins, sets out on his great journey at the behest of Gandalf the wizard, the reader is drawn deep into the wonderful territory of Tolkien's richly-detailed Middle-earth. Like any novel, *The Lord of the Rings* brings with it its baggage of 'content', its social attitudes, whether overtly expressed or murkily implied, but I can think of few examples in the whole of literature where that baggage counts for less when weighed against the book's central attraction. As near as is possible in our unromantic world, Tolkien's masterpiece is pure *story*.

It is as a timeless quest-narrative that the book succeeds: the mysterious portents, the hard travelling, the varied landscapes, the good companionship, the encircling foes, the urgency of the task in hand, the magical revelations – all are handled with a superb sense of story-telling rhythm. It is a slow rhythm, for this is a very long novel, but in its leisurely way it builds a kind of tidal power. The prose is less rich than that of, say, Mervyn Peake or T. H. White – and the characterization is much less original – but the cumulative power of Tolkien's huge tale is undeniable. The atmospheric decorations which all Tolkien cultists find so beguiling – namely the interpolated verses, the invented languages, the obsessively complicated genealogies and mythologies – are of less importance than the simple grandeur of the plot, the imaginary world and the story-telling dynamics. John Ronald Reuel Tolkien (1892–1973) continued to embroider his fantasies of Middle-earth throughout his long life. The results have been published in *The Silmarillion* (1977) and several other posthumous volumes edited by the author's son, Christopher Tolkien. But, whatever their scholarly brilliance, these later books lack the central quality which vitalizes *The Lord of the Rings*: that sense of raw story, in all its glorious primitiveness.

First edition: London, Allen & Unwin, 1954–5 (hardcovers)
First American edition: Boston, Houghton Mifflin, 1954–5 (hardcovers)
Most recent editions: London, Unwin, and New York, Ballantine (paperbacks)

17

WILLIAM GOLDING

Pincher Martin

'He was struggling in every direction, he was the centre of the writhing and kicking knot of his own body. There was no up or down, no light and no air . . .' Golding's third novel may be read as a Posthumous Fantasy – that is, a tale not so much of the afterlife as of the moment of death. I have borrowed this useful term from the critic John Clute. In his review of J. G. Ballard's *The Unlimited Dream Company* (*Foundation* 19, June 1980), he wrote: 'What I'd like to designate the posthumous fantasy, though a better term may well be forthcoming, closely resembles stories like Ambrose Bierce's 'An Occurrence at Owl Creek Bridge', or Conrad Aiken's 'Mr Arcularis', stories where men at the literal point of death escape into an imagined alternative to that death, only gradually to realize that this dream world is fading out, generally to the tune of some insistent horrifying rhythm, perhaps that of the failing heart.' Golding's book fits this paradigm exactly.

Its protagonist, Lieutenant Christopher Martin (known as 'Pincher' to his naval fellows), is a British sailor who is on the point of drowning in the Atlantic Ocean. This is during World War II, and his ship has just been torpedoed by a German U-boat. We seem to enter Martin's consciousness and to follow his thoughts and feelings in minute detail as he struggles against the cold sea. For the first twenty pages of the novel he is adrift, flailing madly, gulping salt water, his mind a confusion of memories, hopes and regrets. No rescue comes, but he spies a small scrap of land, a solitary rock strewn with seaweed, and it proves to be his (temporary) salvation. He hauls himself ashore on this 'single point of rock, peak of a mountain range, one tooth set in the ancient jaw of a sunken world, projecting through the inconceivable vastness of the whole ocean' – and there he remains for the duration of the novel: a man alone, symbol of all the terror of the human condition.

Little happens, but the writing is extraordinarily vivid. As in other books by Golding, we become privileged voyeurs, spying on God's preternaturally bright creation. It is as though we are witnessing everything through the effects of a mind-enhancing drug. We follow poor Pincher Martin as he climbs to the summit of his barren islet, as he searches for food and drink and shelter, and as he stares into the abyss of himself. He is a sort of pared-down, minimal Robinson Crusoe. He holds imaginary conversations with old acquaintances, fights off madness, and suffers occasional delusions of grandeur: '"I am Atlas. I am Prometheus." He felt himself loom, gigantic on the rock.' But in the end he can find no peace, no heavenly grace. The entire hallucination of survival by naked will-power crumbles, and he reverts to what he is: a drowning sailor, soon to be dead.

William Golding (born 1911) is Britain's most recent recipient of the Nobel Prize for Literature. Much of his work is allegorical in nature and takes the form of the historical novel, or science fiction, or (as in this case) metaphysical fantasy. Another of his finest novels is *The Spire* (1964), which concerns the driving obsession of a medieval churchman who wishes to build a 400-foot cathedral spire – ostensibly to the greater glory of God, but possibly to the advantage of the Devil. Like *Pincher Martin*, but more overtly, it deals with the ever-present problem of the evil which dwells in the human heart.

First edition: London, Faber & Faber, 1956 (hardcover)
First American edition: New York, Harcourt Brace, 1957 (as *The Two Deaths of Christopher Martin*; hardcover)
Most recent editions: London, Faber, and New York, Harcourt Brace Jovanovich (paperbacks)

18

RICHARD MATHESON

The Shrinking Man

A year after this novel first appeared as a paperback original it was filmed by Jack Arnold under the catchpenny title of *The Incredible Shrinking Man*. The movie was a minor hit, and reprints of Matheson's book have tended to bear the word 'Incredible' on the cover ever since. This is ironic, for Matheson's chief strength is in fact the degree of credibility which he brings to his elaboration on an absurd premise. Forget about that cloud of radioactive spray which starts the hero off on his inexorable shrinking course; it is nothing but a perfunctory 'sci-fi' pretext for what is fundamentally a potent psychological fantasy. Enjoy the believable domestic details which follow, as the protagonist finds he is no longer a man to his wife and eventually becomes a scurrying insect beneath her feet. The whole thing is like a Kafka fable in an Ideal Homes Exhibition setting.

While on a boating holiday, Scott Carey is exposed to radiation. A few weeks later he begins to lose weight – and height. He makes repeated visits to the doctor before breaking the news to his wife. She is aghast: '*Shrinking*? . . . But that's impossible.' Carey confirms that it is true: 'It's not just my height I'm losing. Every part of me seems to be shrinking. Proportionately.' Already he is down from six feet to five feet eight inches in height. As the days pass, he continues to shrink steadily. He undergoes numerous medical tests, but the doctors remain mystified. Children in the street begin to mistake him for another kid, and he is forced to resign from his job while his wife goes out to work: 'he stood by her side, arm around her back, wanting to comfort her but able only to look up at her face and struggle futilely against the depleted feeling he had at being so much shorter than she.' It is as though he is reverting to infancy, his wife becoming a mother-figure.

However, Carey has not lost his adult sexual urges. When his wife rejects his advances, he feels 'puny and absurd beside her, a ludicrous midget who had planned the seduction of a normal woman.' As he shrinks to less than two feet in height, his frustration grows. He spies on a teenage girl who helps around the house, but panics when she sees him – and runs away like a naughty child. He enjoys a brief friendship with a female circus midget, but even she grows to be a giantess beside him. Soon he is a mere seven inches tall, and living in a doll's house which his wife has thoughtfully provided. One day he ventures into the garden, where he is menaced by a huge bird and driven through a broken window into the cellar. From this point on Carey is lost to the world, too small to escape from the cellar – which stretches before him like an unknown terrain, full of dangers – and too puny to make himself heard. He is now entirely on his own, obliged to forage like some Robinson Crusoe beneath the floorboards, terrified of spiders, and ever shrinking. Eventually he is so minuscule that he is able to climb a spider's web and escape once more into the great outdoors. There he finds a sense of peace beneath the stars: he learns to accept his lot, as he shrinks into new worlds of enchantment and possibility.

Richard Matheson (born 1926) is best known nowadays for his film and television work. Since writing the screenplay for *The Incredible Shrinking Man*, he has helped in the creation of many other movies, including Steven Spielberg's remarkable tale of terror *Duel* (1971). But he has continued to write novels, among them a memorable time-slip romance entitled *Bid Time Return* (1975). He is one of America's leading creators of fantasy.

First edition: New York, Fawcett, 1956 (paperback)
First British edition: London, Muller, 1956 (hardcover)
Most recent editions: New York, Bantam, and London, Corgi (paperbacks)

19

RAY BRADBURY

Dandelion Wine

Winesburg, Ohio, becomes the October Country. Or
rather, Green Town, Illinois, during the long hot summer
of 1928, is made over in the feverish imagination of twelve-
year-old Douglas Spaulding – so that it seems to become a
realm of time-travellers and witches and magic, of
enchanted tennis shoes and Rube Goldberg 'happiness
machines'. This is not a fantasy of the supernatural in any
conventional sense, but it is a highly imaginative work
which mines a deep vein of modern American folk-fantasy.
There is much delightful whimsy here, combined with an
obvious yearning for a simpler, old-fashioned way of life.
But there are also darker elements: Douglas realizes that
one day he will die; an old woman is robbed of all the
memories of her youth; a killer known as the Lonely One
lurks in the town's shadows. Like his earlier *The Martian
Chronicles* (1950), this book by Ray Bradbury is a collection
of short stories furbished with linking passges and presented
anew as a novel. And like all Bradbury's work it is very
much about childhood, the child's-eye view of things.

> The grass whispered under his body . . . The wind
> sighed over his shelled ears. The world slipped bright
> over the glassy round of his eyeballs . . . Birds flickered
> like skipped stones across the vast inverted pond of
> heaven . . . Insects shocked the air with electric clearness.
> Ten thousand individual hairs grew a millionth of an inch
> on his head. He heard the twin hearts beating in each ear,
> the third heart beating in his throat, the two hearts

throbbing his wrists, the real heart pounding his chest. The million pores on his body opened.

I'm *really* alive! he thought.

Apart from such all-important revelations, little happens. Douglas helps his grandfather pick the golden-headed flowers which will be used to make Dandelion Wine ('the words were summer on the tongue'). Throughout the months of June, July and August the old man bottles his wine, each bottle like the distilled essence of a summer's day. This is the conceit which unifies the book: a string of days, a row of bottles, yesterday's sunshine trapped. Bradbury's *Dandelion Wine* is a book of memories, a profoundly nostalgic tribute to his own Midwestern boyhood. Its magic is as delicate as a dandelion's 'clock' or seed-bearing head – one touch and it will fly into a thousand fragments. It is difficult to analyse the reasons for its success, but in this volume Bradbury's characteristic blend of poetry, comedy, sentimentality and nostalgia works quite beautifully.

It was to be his last fully satisfactory work, in my opinion. The later fantasy novel *Something Wicked This Way Comes* (1962), which attempts to reuse some of the same childhood material in a more macabre fashion, seems by comparison very repetitive and 'forced'. Ray Douglas Bradbury (born 1920) is a wonderful short-story writer who has never been at ease with the novel form. Apart from the excellent material in *Dandelion Wine*, the best of his fantastic stories are to be found in *The October Country* (1955), a fat collection which contains tales comical, grotesque, horrifying and touching.

First edition: New York, Doubleday, 1957 (hardcover)
First British edition: London, Hart-Davis, 1957 (hardcover)
Most recent editions: New York, Bantam, and London, Grafton (paperbacks)

20

T.H. WHITE

The Once and Future King

This volume contains four novels: *The Sword in the Stone* (1938), *The Queen of Air and Darkness* (formerly *The Witch in the Wood*, 1939), *The Ill-Made Knight* (1940) and *The Candle in the Wind* (published for the first time here). Together they retell the story of King Arthur and his Knights of the Round Table, beginning with Arthur's education at the hands of the wizard Merlyn (so-spelled). There have been countless Arthurian novels, but few which have inspired such devotion as this delightfully humorous and imaginative work. It became a best-seller when published in its final form in 1958, and inspired a Broadway musical, *Camelot*, as well as two films. In his book *Imaginary Worlds* the American novelist and critic Lin Carter states: 'the single finest fantasy novel written in our time, or for that matter, *ever* written, is, must be, by any conceivable standard, T. H. White's *The Once and Future King*.'

It is by no means a straight rendering of the time-honoured tale. Although he sets the narrative in the high Middle Ages, White uses deliberate anachronisms – usually to charming effect, although sometimes the 'modern' references have dated ('Lancelot ended by being the greatest knight King Arthur had. He was a sort of Bradman, top of the battling averages'). He also introduces many supernatural elements, over and above those which are traditional. Young Arthur, or 'the Wart' as he is known, is transformed by Merlyn into various beasts of the field, and is able to fly as a bird or swim as a fish. But the book's main qualities are its realism – White shows remarkable knowledge of sports such as hawking, as well as medieval techniques of hunting, agriculture and warfare – and its strongly expressed feeling for nature. All this is combined with a powerful visual imagination:

> There was a clearing in the forest, a wide sward of moonlit grass, and the white rays shone full upon the tree trunks on the opposite side. These trees were beeches, whose trunks are always more beautiful in a pearly light, and among the beeches there was the smallest movement and a silvery clink. Before the clink there were just the beeches, but immediately afterward there was a knight in full armour, standing still and silent and unearthly, among the majestic trunks. He was mounted on an enormous white horse that stood as rapt as its master, and he carried in his right hand, with its butt resting on the stirrup, a high, smooth jousting lance, which stood up among the tree stumps, higher and higher, till it was outlined against the velvet sky. All was moonlit, all silver, too beautiful to describe.

The book is also notable for its comic characterizations (the knight in the above scene turns out to be a bespectacled twit who starts at the slightest sound). Particularly rich in humour is the portrayal of the brilliant but confused and topsy-turvy Merlyn, who is so intent on remembering the future that he has no knowledge of the past. Matters darken in the later episodes, which deal with Arthur's adulthood and his attempts to rule wisely, and which also recount the tragic love of Queen Guenever for Sir Lancelot. But the magic of this author's light touch remains potent throughout. Terence Hanbury White (1906–64) wrote a number of other books, including *Mistress Masham's Repose* (1947), a fantasy novel about a girl who discovers a lost colony of Gulliver's Lilliputians living on an island in a lake. A posthumously published work, *The Book of Merlyn* (1977), serves as an entertaining addendum to *The Once and Future King*.

First edition: London, Collins, 1958 (hardcover)
First American edition: New York, Putnam, 1958 (hardcover)
Most recent editions: London, Fontana, and New York, Berkley (paperbacks)

21

ROBERT A. HEINLEIN

The Unpleasant Profession of Jonathan Hoag

I cheat slightly by including this book in a list of the hundred best fantasy novels. 'The Unpleasant Profession of Jonathan Hoag' is a 105-page novella which takes pride of place in a volume of six stories by Robert Heinlein (1907–88). It was first published in *Unknown Worlds* in 1942, and is surely one of the most entertaining things ever to have appeared in that much-praised magazine.

The leading characters, Teddy and Cynthia Randall, are a husband-and-wife team of private detectives. Like such Hollywood contemporaries as Nick and Nora Charles or Mr and Mrs North, they indulge in continuous good-humoured banter (one would suspect that Heinlein wrote this story with the movies in mind, were it not for the probably unfilmable ending). They are very much in love. One evening they receive a new client, a fussy little man named Jonathan Hoag, who is distressed by a mysterious reddish substance, possibly dried blood, which he has found under his fingernails. Hoag wants the Randalls to follow him in the daytime and to find out what his profession is – for he has no memory of his own work; his days from nine to five are a complete blank to him. He is willing to pay generously, so Teddy and Cynthia are glad to accept this extremely odd assignment. Next morning, Teddy Randall shadows Mr Hoag and establishes to his own satisfaction that the man works as a gem-polisher on the thirteenth floor of a certain office block. The red substance beneath his fingernails must have been jeweller's rouge. However, when Randall attempts to show Cynthia the offices in question, he finds that there *is* no thirteenth floor, nor is there a jewellery company in the building. Randall seems to be suffering from a delusion – possibly he has been hypnotized – and, unfortunately, he remains in the dark as to the nature of Hoag's profession.

Matters become much stranger. In a dream, Randall is hauled before a bizarre board-meeting of businessmen who call themselves The Sons of the Bird. They warn him against any dealings with Mr Jonathan Hoag. On awakening, he discounts this experience, and continues his fruitless efforts to penetrate the Hoag mystery. However, the Sons of the Bird turn out to be all too real. They inhabit a looking-glass realm, but they are also capable of entering our workaday world. By means of mirrors, they capture both Randall and his wife and subject them to various torments before returning them to their apartment. After this ordeal Cynthia does not wake up, for her soul has been retained by the Sons of the Bird. Randall is driven close to despair before realizing that he has one firm ally he can turn to for help – namely Jonathan Hoag, that oddly meek little man whom the Sons of The Bird clearly detest and fear. No doubt they have good reason to fear him, especially if he should regain his memory. When at last it is revealed, Hoag's line of work proves to be something comically unexpected – and the story reaches a fine pitch of madness before its apocalyptic conclusion.

'The Unpleasant Profession of Jonathan Hoag' is quite untypical of most of Heinlein's other fiction of the period (which tended to be hard science fiction of the near-future variety). It is an absurd piece, with a number of flaws in its logic, but it is also a pleasing *jeu d'esprit*.

First edition: New York, Gnome Press, 1959 (hardcover)
First British edition: London, Dobson, 1964 (hardcover)
Most recent editions: New York, Berkley, and London, NEL (paperbacks)

22

SHIRLEY JACKSON

The Haunting of Hill House

Dr John Montague, an anthropologist with an interest in the supernatural, invites three people to spend a few days with him in Hill House, a now empty country residence which has a reputation for being haunted and which he has leased for a short term. The courageous trio consists of Eleanor Vance, a 32-year-old spinster who has recently been enjoying a new sense of freedom (and guilt?) following the death of her valetudinarian mother; Theodora, or 'Theo', an artistically inclined young woman who lives in a city apartment with her companion (sex unspecified); and Luke Sanderson, the charming but ne'er-do-well nephew of Hill House's absent owner. Eleanor and Theodora have both had previous experiences of the paranormal; Luke is there merely as an observer. None of these people has seen Hill House, and each is suitably depressed by the place when he or she arrives:

No human eye can isolate the unhappy coincidence of line and place which suggests evil in the face of a house, and yet somehow a maniac juxtaposition, a badly turned angle, some chance meeting of roof and sky, turned Hill House into a place of despair, more frightening because the face of Hill House seemed awake, with a watchfulness from the blank windows and a touch of glee in the eyebrow of a cornice . . . It was a house without kindness, never meant to be lived in, not a fit place for people or for love or for hope. Exorcism cannot alter the countenance of a house; Hill House would stay as it was until it was destroyed.

I should have turned back at the gate, Eleanor thought.

Nevertheless the guests determine to brave it out. Strangers to each other, they soon find that they are pleased with each other's company. They indulge in games and repartee, mild flirtations and rivalries. Dr Montague's little 'experiment' becomes an enjoyable adventure, particularly for the repressed Eleanor. But supernatural manifestations do begin to occur – self-closing doors, mysterious icy draughts, banging noises in the night, messages scrawled on walls – and an atmosphere of subdued terror mounts.

The entity which haunts Hill House has a particular interest in Eleanor Vance, leaving such messages as 'HELP ELEANOR COME HOME ELEANOR' in red letters above her bed. Events progress towards a wrenching climax which I shall not divulge here. One of the achievements of this very subtle supernatural-horror story is the way in which it suggests that one can be all alone and extremely frightened even when one is surrounded by apparently friendly and sympathetic people. It is a psychologically acute novel, one in which the action flows logically and remorselessly from character. It contains no obvious villains. Stephen King has correctly commented: 'it is the character of Eleanor and Shirley Jackson's depiction of it that elevates *The Haunting of Hill House* into the ranks of the great supernatural novels.' We could go so far as to assert, as King has done in his *Danse Macabre*, that the author is almost a match for Henry James in his *Turn of the Screw* vein. This is high praise indeed. Yet, despite all the carefully implied psychological machinery and the variety of possible explanations for the outcome of the plot, the supernatural elements in *The Haunting of Hill House* are 'real': that is to say, the novel is undoubtedly a fantasy. Shirley Jackson (1919–65) was a highly talented American writer of macabre short stories and novels, and this book is her masterpiece.

First edition: New York, Viking, 1959 (hardcover)
First British edition: London, Michael Joseph, 1960
(hardcover)
Most recent editions: New York, Penguin, and London,
Robinson (paperbacks)

23

MERVYN PEAKE

Titus Alone

The third and last of Peake's novels about Titus Groan is, and always will be, a 'problem' book. It is considerably shorter than its predecessors (*1*, *10*), and the narrative rhythm feels quite different. It is divided into brief splintery chapters, many of which appear to be incomplete. Much of the dialogue sparkles and some of the episodes are brilliantly imaginative, but other passages seem inconsequential. The revised second edition (1970) carries an explanatory note by the editor, Langdon Jones: 'Mervyn Peake was already suffering from his final illness at the time of submission . . . My aim has been to incorporate all Peake's own corrections while ignoring all other alterations. It has also been to try to make the book as consistent as possible with the minimum of my own alterations . . . Had Peake been able to continue there is no doubt that he would have polished the story still more.' (In the last decade of his life Peake suffered tragically from a degenerative disease.)

Gormenghast ended with Titus saying farewell to his mother and riding out into the wide world. His mother had warned: 'There is nowhere else . . . You will only tread a circle, Titus Groan. There's not a road, not a track, but it will lead you home. For everything comes to Gormenghast.' Now we are to follow the hero on his momentous journey, and learn whether this prophecy is true. At the beginning of *Titus Alone* he arrives, exhausted and wet, at a riverbank on the outskirts of a great city – and there he meets a man called Muzzlehatch who drives an automobile: 'a long shadowy car approached with a screech out of the gloom. Its bonnet was the colour of blood. Its water was boiling. It snorted like a horse and shook itself as though it were alive.' Titus is dumped in the back seat and carried away: 'the car backfired with such violence that a dog turned over in its sleep four miles away, and then, with an upheaval that lifted the bonnet of the car and brought it down again with a crash of metal, the wild thing shook itself as though bent upon its own destruction, shook itself, roared, and leapt forward and away down tortuous alleys still wet and black with the night shadows.' This passage comes as a surprise to readers of the previous novels – it indicates that we are firmly in the modern world, in a city-terrain of machines, speed and noise which is utterly alien to the slow movements and immemorial technologies of pre-industrial Gormenghast.

But it is not quite *our* world that the hero has arrived in. At times, the story reads like avant-garde science fiction, for Titus soon encounters yet more fantastic machines. Deep within the city, aircraft and robotic devices litter a landscape of futuristic architecture. Strange, helmeted men pursue him, and he falls through the glass roof of a huge building into the midst of an animated party. He becomes embroiled in a love affair, is arrested, and goes to court. The eccentric Muzzlehatch comes to his rescue again and again, but Titus continues to find himself in trouble. He penetrates the weird realm known as the Under-River, peopled by bizarre and menacing characters. The events of the novel become more and more phantasmagoric, and all the while Titus is haunted by memories of his unique past, a past which no one else can comprehend or even believe in. Although overwhelmed by homesickness, in the end he escapes from the city but does not return home. There is no need, for he has come to realize that he carries his Gormenghast within him.

First edition: London, Eyre & Spottiswoode, 1959 (hardcover)
First American edition: New York, Weybright & Talley, 1967 (hardcover)
Most recent edition: London, Methuen (paperback)

24

PETER S. BEAGLE

A Fine and Private Place

The seventeenth-century English poet Andrew Marvell wrote: 'The grave's a fine and private place, But none I think do there embrace.' In this wayward novel of love and death, two of the characters try to challenge Marvell's truth. The New York-born writer Peter Beagle was just twenty-one years old when he published his wryly amusing (and sometimes poetic) tale of the supernatural. It opens in Yorkchester Cemetery, New York, where an erstwhile drugstore proprietor named Mr Jonathan Rebeck has made his home. Having retired from the world, and feeling a closer affinity with the dead than with the living, he now sleeps in a small mausoleum. He never leaves the cemetery, where he enjoys the companionship of the local ghosts and an unlikely talking raven (the bird keeps Mr Rebeck supplied with titbits of food). Among those he befriends is the unhappy ghost of Michael, a 34-year-old man who has been murdered by his wife. We see Michael returning to consciousness during his funeral, and later he escapes his coffin but finds that he is unable to leave the graveyard:

> It took him a while to realize that he had left his grave, and when he did it didn't seem very important. I'm out, he said to himself, and I can talk again and move around, and I'm no better off than I was. Alive, he could at least have kept up the pretence of having somewhere to go; but now he could just sit by the roadside for the next few million years, if he felt like it . . .
>
> There was no stone yet, only a small metal marker. It

said: 'Michael Morgan, March 7, 1924–June 10, 1958', and he felt very pleased with its conciseness . . . My body is there, he thought. All my chicken dinners and head-scratching and sneezing and fornication and hot baths and sunburns and beer and shaving – all buried and forgotten. All the little pettinesses washed away.

Michael plays chess and discusses the way of the world with Mr Rebeck, but, being a mere phantasm, he has no appetites and cannot sleep. In time they are joined by another ghost, an attractive but spinsterish young woman named Laura, who moves 'like a dandelion plume on a day wrinkled with small winds, barely touching the ground'. The two ghostly people grow to love each other but, alas, they are unable to touch: 'There was a point in space where their hands, thin as breath, met and seemed to become one hand, through which the sun shone and a leaf fell.' However, the fleshly Mr Rebeck also finds a female companion – from among the living. Gertrude Klapper, a handsome middle-aged widow, becomes acquainted with the old recluse when she visits her husband's grave. Rebeck begins to warm to her, for she is a good-hearted, expansive Jewish lady (the most fully rounded character in the novel) and sorely in need of companionship. Gradually, she draws him out – and Rebeck, moved by the plight of the unfortunate Michael and Laura, decides to leave his 'fine and private place' and embrace the living. This light fantasia by Peter S. Beagle (born 1939) is talky, sentimental and often lyrical. It also has great charm, and is a remarkable achievement for an author who was barely out of his teens at the time of its composition.

First edition: New York, Viking, 1960 (hardcover)
First British edition: London, Muller, 1961 (hardcover)
Most recent editions: New York, Del Rey, and London, Unwin (paperbacks)

25

POUL ANDERSON

Three Hearts and Three Lions

This very enjoyable fantasy is in a a rather different vein from the same author's *The Broken Sword* (*15*), although it was written soon after the other, having been serialized in the *Magazine of Fantasy and Science Fiction* in 1953. The light-hearted story of a modern man who is plunged into a world of medieval romance, it has much in common with de Camp and Pratt's tales of Harold Shea, the 'incomplete enchanter' (*7*). The hero, Holger Carlsen, is an American-educated Dane who returns to his homeland in order to join the underground struggle against the Nazi occupiers during World War II. He is knocked unconscious during a desperate hand-to-hand fight – and awakes to find himself in a different universe.

By mysterious means, he has been transported to a land of Carolingian myth, a world of bold knights, beautiful damsels, foul witches and fire-breathing dragons. Charlemagne's empire still stands, with the Saracens to the south and the realms of Faerie to the east. It seems that Holger has been brought here according to some deliberate plan: he is alone in a wood, but a fine steed awaits him, together with weapons and a suit of perfectly-fitting armour. When he removes the canvas cover from his shield, he sees that it bears 'a design of three golden lions alternating with three red hearts on a blue background'. He has little choice but to take up these accoutrements, mount the horse, and ride off in search of information. A friendly witch gives him shelter for the night and advises him to seek his fortune in the land of Faerie. She also introduces him to an unlikely guide – a three-foot dwarf named Hugi who seems to speak in Scots dialect: 'Come on, come on, ma knichtly loon, let's na stay the day . . . Who fares to Faerie maun ride a swift steed.'

Holger and Hugi ride into the enchanted land of Faerie, where many adventures await them. On the way, they meet a lovely young swan-maiden, Alianora, who becomes their travelling companion. The perils come thick and fast: Duke Alfric of Faerie attempts to trick Holger into a hundred-year snooze beneath a hill; Morgan le Fay, who has 'a body with more curves than a scenic highway', tries to seduce him; a dragon attacks them, but Holger defeats it by casting water down its gullet ('a little thermodynamics is all,' he explains casually. 'Caused a small boiler explosion'); they have run-ins with giants, trolls, and other tricky creatures – but, with Hugi's and Alianora's help, Holger wins through. The purpose of his quest becomes clear: he has been brought to this world to help the forces of Law defeat those of Chaos. He is Holger Danske, or Ogier le Danois, fabled in the Carolingian chronicles as a champion who is fated to return again and again . . .

Three Hearts and Three Lions is an entertaining tale of a type which has become exceedingly familiar in the past couple of decades but has rarely been done so well. The humour, romance and derring-do are all nicely balanced, the invention is profuse, and the whole is neatly wrapped up in just 160 pages. It is a pity that most of the multi-volume fantasy epics of recent years cannot show a comparable degree of wit and economy.

First edition: New York, Doubleday, 1961 (hardcover)
First British edition: London, Sphere, 1973 (paperback)
Most recent edition: New York, Avon (paperback)

26

JOHN D. MacDONALD

The Girl, the Gold Watch, and Everything

'If Thorne Smith and Mickey Spillane had collaborated,' suggests the paperback blurb, they would have produced something very like this book. John Dann MacDonald (1916–86) was best known as a writer of crime thrillers, and particularly celebrated for his seductive series of 'Travis McGee' adventures, which began with *The Deep Blue Goodbye* in 1964. He had produced a couple of science fiction novels early in his career, but *The Girl, The Gold Watch, and Everything* was his only full-length fantasy.

The hero, Kirby Winter, is a 32-year-old wimp who, despite his good looks, is terrified of women. He works as a roving philanthropist for his eccentric uncle, a former schoolmaster who has discovered a secret source of immense wealth. For some eleven years it has been Kirby's task to give away vast quantities of money on his uncle's behalf. He has been doing this more or less unquestioningly, travelling the world with an open chequebook – and dogged by a continuing sense of his own sexual inadequacy. Every time he comes close to consummating a love affair, something goes badly wrong: an earthquake strikes, or he takes some ludicrous pratfall. The story opens just after Uncle Omar's death, when Kirby finds that he has inherited nothing but an old-fashioned gold pocket-watch.

No sooner is the old man dead and buried than all hell breaks loose. The tax authorities want to know what has *really* happened to the twenty-seven million dollars which Kirby claims to have given away; meanwhile, various crooks are moving in, all ferociously keen to discover the source of Uncle Omar's riches. Kirby finds himself being chased by various beautiful women, some of whom have ulterior motives for seeking his company. 'The Girl' of the novel's title is, however, a complete innocent (much like Kirby himself) – a gorgeous country bumpkin called Bonny Lee, who accidentally crawls into bed with Kirby one night, mistaking him for her regular lover, and thus introduces herself in the most memorable fashion possible. Following this diverting episode Kirby at last comes into his own as a hero, and, with Bonny Lee at his side, he discovers the true nature of his uncle's legacy. The gold watch contains the secret: it is a device for controlling time. When Kirby twists a certain knob, time freezes; the world seems to enter a red-lit stasis, and he is able to move around for up to one subjective hour, rearranging people and things to his own satisfaction. It is a magical invention which confers immense power on its owner, and it should at the very least enable Kirby and Bonny Lee to extricate themselves from all their difficulties.

MacDonald's novel is an amusing romp, part sex-comedy, part alarming power-fantasy. The love scenes now seem dated and coy, and the pratfalls in the first half of the book come too thick and fast to be truly funny; but the story springs to life in the second half, once the characters enter the enchanted world of the watch. The basic idea (or something very like it) had already been used by H. G. Wells in his short story 'The New Accelerator' (1901), but MacDonald works out many of its implications at length in this efficient and pleasurable entertainment – without forgetting to point the moral that life would be quite intolerable if such a cruelly manipulative device really did exist.

First edition: New York, Fawcett, 1962 (paperback)
First British edition: London, Coronet, 1968 (paperback)
Most recent edition: New York, Fawcett (paperback)

27

ROBERT A. HEINLEIN

Glory Road

Heinlein was the doyen of American science fiction writers, particularly noted for his hard-headed, not to say hard-nosed, depiction of near-future technological developments. Yet, as we have already seen in respect of *The Unpleasant Profession of Jonathan Hoag* (21), he also had a penchant for fantasy. In old age, he produced a number of novels which are more fantasy than sf, a recent example being the James Branch Cabell-influenced *Job: A Comedy of Justice* (1984). The first, and perhaps the most popular, of his late-period fantasies was *Glory Road* – an attempt to produce a good-natured, swinging, *Unknown*-style swash-buckler for the sixties, an escapist romp which evokes a world 'where there is no smog and no parking problem and no population explosion . . . no Cold War and no H-bombs and no television commercials . . . no Summit Conferences, no Foreign Aid, no hidden taxes – no income tax'.

The hero, E. C. 'Scar' Gordon, is a tough, flippant American soldier who is wounded while serving as a 'military adviser' in South-East Asia. Still in his early twenties, he decides to leave the army and take a European university degree in order to set himself up for the good life back home. While lounging on a nudist beach in the South of France, he meets a gorgeous (and well-muscled) blonde girl who astonishes him by saying: 'You are very beautiful.' He is so amazed by the remark that he forgets to ask for her name and number. Obsessed with this young woman, and depressed at the state of the world (like his creator, he has robustly right-wing, 'libertarian' views), Gordon decides that a safe middle-class career will not suit him after all:

> I didn't want to go back to school . . . I no longer gave a damn about three-car garages and swimming pools, nor any other status symbol or 'security'. There was *no* security in this world and only damn fools and mice thought there could be.
>
> Somewhere back in the jungle I had shucked off all ambition of that sort. I had been shot at too many times and had lost interest in supermarkets and exurban subdivisions and tonight is the PTA supper don't forget dear you promised . . .
>
> I wanted a Roc's egg . . . I wanted the hurtling moons of Barsoom. I wanted Storisende and Poictesme, and Holmes shaking me awake to tell me, 'The game's afoot!' . . . I wanted Prester John, and Excalibur held by a moon-white arm out of a silent lake . . .

(For a young jock of the early 1960s, he has read a surprising quantity of yesteryear's romantic fiction.) Unable to find his nude 'Helen of Troy' once more, he answers a newspaper advertisement which calls for a fit male proficient with all weapons and indomitably courageous – and it turns out that the advertiser is none other than his beautiful blonde temptress. It seems that she is in need of a champion: 'There will be great adventure . . . and greater treasure.' Besotted young Gordon leaps at the chance, and soon finds himself whisked away, via a 'pentacle of power', to another world – a world fit for heroes heroines and monsters. What follows is an extremely jolly sword-and-sorcery yarn, full of wisecracks, folksy apothegms, low comedy, mild sexual titillation, references to popular literature, and exciting (if far-fetched) action. The telling counts for more than the tale, the manner is more important than the matter. Heinlein's voice may be too intrusive for some readers – but for the large audience which is susceptible to his rather hectoring charm this book reveals the author near the top of his form.

First edition: New York, Avon, 1963 (paperback)
First British edition: London, Four Square, 1965 (paperback)
Most recent editions: New York, Ace, and London, NEL (paperbacks)

28

ANDRE NORTON

Witch World

'Andre Norton' is Alice Mary Norton (born 1912), a popular American author of books for young people. She began by writing historical fiction and thrillers during the thirties and forties, then turned to sf and fantasy in the early fifties. Although she did not make her name in the magazines, she is essentially a pulp writer in the garish tradition of Edgar Rice Burroughs and Robert E. Howard. *Witch World* was the first novel in a series which has become her most highly regarded work, enjoyed by adults as well as teenagers and usually reprinted without any tell-tale 'juvenile' packaging. Later titles in the sequence include *Web of the Witch World* (1964), *Year of the Unicorn* (1965), *Three Against the Witch World* (1965), *Warlock of the Witch World* (1967), *Sorceress of the Witch World* (1968), *Spell of the Witch World* (short stories, 1972), *The Crystal Gryphon* (1972) and so on.

It is basically a sword-and-sorcery series, even if it is not labelled as such. The first of these books is the tale of a man, a World War II veteran named Simon Tregarth, who is projected by magic into the rugged terrain of a mysterious parallel world. There he helps save the life of a young witch, and subsequently becomes a soldier on behalf of her beleaguered people. Much hard travelling and many arduous battles follow, before he wins his lady's hand – and at last learns her name:

'Simon, my name is Jaelithe.'
It came so abruptly, that for a full moment he did not

understand her meaning. And then, knowing the Estcarpian custom, of the rules which had bound her so long, he drew a deep breath of wonder at her complete surrender: her name, that most personal possession in the realm of the Power, which must never be yielded lest one yield with it one's own identity to another!

Norton is a vigorous and inventive story-teller whose prose style, if unlovely, is (as they say) serviceable.

Although Andre Norton adopted a masculine pseudonym, and although her hero in this book is male, the most notable feature of the *Witch World* series is the position of moral and political power which it gives to the women of its imagined society. 'Estcarp' is a matriarchal society, run by a coven of good witches whose magical talents enable their warriors to repulse the encircling enemies. 'The power of the women of Estcarp was legendary,' as an envious character observes. Later, one of the male soldiers explains to Simon: 'We have the greatest reverence for the Women of Power. But it is in the nature of their lives that they are apart from us, and the things which may move us. For, as you know, the Power departs from a witch if she becomes truly a woman. Therefore they are doubly jealous of their strength, having given up a part of their life to hold it. Also they are proud that they are women.'

This proto-feminist aspect of the *Witch World* series has no doubt contributed to the popularity of Norton's books with female readers. She has also exerted a strong influence on later women writers of fantasy and fantasy-tinged science fiction – among those who could be said to belong to an 'Andre Norton tradition' are Marion Zimmer Bradley, with her Darkover series, and Anne McCaffrey, with her Dragonriders novels. In a genre which long ago became overpopulated with loutish male barbarians, Norton's example was refreshing and benign.

First edition: New York, Ace, 1963 (paperback)
First British edition: London, Tandem, 1970 (paperback)
Most recent editions: New York, Ace, and London, VGSF (paperbacks)

29

JOHN FOWLES

The Magus

Can *The Magus* be regarded as a fantasy novel? By and large, its mysteries are rationalized, the apparently supernatural elements explained away. Yet it is certainly a fable of the extraordinary, and very much a book about magic and illusion. As the author acknowledges in his introduction to the 1977 edition, the novel was influenced by the psychology of Jung, as well as by that haunting tale of an adolescent *rite de passage*, Alain-Fournier's *Le Grand Meaulnes* (1913; translated as *The Lost Domain*). Fowles's original title for the book, and one whose rejection he still sometimes regrets, was *The Godgame*.

Nicholas Urfe, a hollow young Englishman, is on the run from love and adult responsibilities. He goes to teach at the Lord Byron School in the Greek islands: 'Phraxos lay eight dazzling hours in a small steamer south of Athens . . . It took my breath away when I first saw it, floating under Venus like a majestic black whale in an amethyst evening sea . . . Its beauty was rare even in the Aegean, because its hills were covered with pine trees, Mediterranean pines as light as greenfinch feathers. Nine-tenths of the island was uninhabited and uncultivated: nothing but pines, coves, silence, sea.' In this lonely setting, described with ravishing intensity throughout the novel, Urfe meets a remarkable old man named Conchis. The latter lives with his house-keeper in a villa overlooking the sea. It is full of books, paintings, musical instruments, objets d'art. Conchis is evidently a man of great intelligence and refinement; he tells Urfe wonderful stories of his experiences during the early years of the century, and of his love-life. He also claims to be a 'psychic' and a 'traveller in other worlds'.

Before long, uncanny events begin to occur. Urfe hears mysterious music, and finds clues which point to another, hidden, inhabitant of the villa. A lovely young woman, the image of Conchis's long-lost girlfriend who died in 1916, appears by night. Now Urfe is being inducted into the Godgame, but it will be a long time before he comes to understand its nature. Is Conchis a magician, the Prospero of this island, or is he an extremely cunning practical joker? Is he indulging in some cruel and nefarious sport, or is he a guru of unlimited wisdom who will lead Urfe towards a new sense of meaning in his life? Whatever the case, the young man is invigorated by all that takes place: 'as I walked there came the strangest feeling, compounded of the early hour, the absolute solitude, and what had happened, of having entered a myth; a knowledge of what it was like physically, moment by moment, to have been young and ancient, a Ulysses on his way to meet Circe, a Theseus on his journey to Crete, an Oedipus still searching for his destiny.'

The hero becomes eager to plunge deeper into the mysteries posed by Conchis – even if horrors await him (as they do). The reader is eager too, for this long novel of some 650 pages becomes almost impossible to put down. It is one of the most engrossing reading experiences in modern fiction, a psychological mystery which is also a magnificent piece of story-telling. John Fowles (born 1926) achieved a deserved success with *The Magus*, which became the object of a cult among younger readers. Unfortunately, the 1968 film version, with Michael Caine as Urfe and Anthony Quinn as Conchis, was a poor thing. Fowles's later book *A Maggot* (1986) – part historical novel, part science fiction – is also an outstanding work of the fantastic imagination.

First edition: Boston, Little, Brown, 1965 (hardcover)
First British edition: London, Cape, 1966 (hardcover)
Most recent editions: New York, Dell, and London, Grafton (paperbacks).

30

MICHAEL MOORCOCK

Stormbringer

'Elric rode like a giant scarecrow, gaunt and rigid on the massive back of the Nihrainian steed. His grim face was set fast in a mask that hid emotion and his crimson eyes burned like coals in their sunken sockets. The wind whipped his hair this way and that, but he sat straight, staring ahead, one long-fingered hand gripping *Stormbringer*'s hilt.' This frequently ironic and moody sword-and-sorcery epic was the first published novel by a man who has become one of Britain's major writers of fiction, famous for his outrageous imagination, his anarchism, and his guru-like influence on younger authors. Michael Moorcock (born 1939) invented the red-eyed, albino warrior Elric of Melniboné for *Science Fantasy* magazine in 1961. A collection of Elric's adventures appeared in book form as *The Stealer of Souls* (1963), to be followed by this novel and several more volumes: *The Singing Citadel* (1970), *The Sleeping Sorceress* (1971), *Elric of Melniboné* (1972) and *The Sailor on the Seas of Fate* (1976), among others. Despite its relatively early appearance, *Stormbringer* is the climactic book of the series, the tale which brings the doom-laden saga of Elric to its close.

Moorcock's friend J. G. Ballard wrote a lengthy endorsement for the dust-jacket of the first edition: 'strange and tormented landscapes, peopled by characters of archetypal dimensions, are the setting for a series of titanic duels between the forces of Chaos and Order. Nightmare armies clash on the shores of spectral seas. Phantom horsemen ride on skeleton steeds across a world as fantastic as those of Bosch and Breughel. Over all these presides the central figure of Elric, the haunted warrior-king whose ambivalent relationship with the magical sword Stormbringer is the author's most original creation. The vast, tragic and sometimes terrifying symbols by which Mr Moorcock continually illuminates the metaphysical quest of his hero are a measure of the author's remarkable talents.' It is a somewhat flattering description, but it nevertheless captures the essence of this impetuous, headlong, half-mad book.

Elric is a comparative weakling without his sword, the half-sentient 'rune-blade' Stormbringer. It drinks the life-force from its victims, conferring on Elric tremendous strength and vitality. This does not make the hero happy: he hates his weapon (as it apparently hates him), yet the two are inseparable. At the beginning of the novel Elric has put the sword aside, and is attempting to rule his kingdom in peace. However, the supernatural minions of some evil master kidnap his wife, Zarozinia, and Elric is obliged to grasp Stormbringer once more. He soon becomes involved in world-shaking events: the forces of Chaos have broken loose, and everything is about to fall into wrack and ruin. With his faithful henchman Moonglum, Elric travels far and wide, encountering one terrible foe after another. All this is narrated speedily, and with great relish on the author's part. The story mounts from one climax to another, each surpassing the preceding one in sound and fury. Elric tackles the Counts of Hell, and eventually finds Zarozinia – only to lose her again. She is transformed into a wormlike creature, and, in a memorably horrid scene, she impales herself on her husband's magic blade. Events move on to a final grandiose climax, in which Elric goes to meet his death, even as his world is torn apart and a new universe is born.

First edition: London, Jenkins, 1965 (hardcover)
First American edition: New York, Lancer, 1967 (paperback)
Most recent editions: London, Grafton, and New York, Berkley (paperbacks)

31

THOMAS PYNCHON

The Crying of Lot 49

Thomas Pynchon (born 1937) has a formidable literary reputation, largely based on work which he did while still in his twenties. *The Crying of Lot 49* is the shortest and most accessible of his three novels. The other two are *V* (1963) and *Gravity's Rainbow* (1973), both of which have been described as 'post-modernist' fabulations – as are the majority of the books by those American novelists most commonly associated with Pynchon: John Barth (*Giles Goat-Boy*, 1966), Donald Barthelme (*The Dead Father*, 1975) and Robert Coover (*The Public Burning*, 1977). *Lot 49* is the bizarre story of a young woman called Oedipa Maas, who finds that she has been named executor of the tangled estate of Pierce Inverarity, her former lover and 'a California real estate mogul'. She falls in with a shyster lawyer, a pop group called The Paranoids, and various other weird characters (who have names such as Doctor Hilarius and Genghis Cohen). She discovers a secret, underground postal system known as W.A.S.T.E. or Trystero, its symbol a muted posthorn, and from this point on things get stranger and stranger. Oedipa comes across the posthorn motif everywhere:

In Chinatown, in the dark window of a herbalist, she thought she saw it on a sign among ideographs. But the streetlight was dim. Later, on a sidewalk, she saw two of them in chalk, 20 feet apart . . .
    In the buses all night she listened to transistor radios playing songs in the lower stretches of the Top 200 . . .

A Mexican girl, trying to hear one of these through snarling static from the bus's motor, hummed along as if she would remember it always, tracing posthorns and hearts with a fingernail, in the haze of her breath on the window.

An obscure Jacobean revenge play, *The Courier's Tragedy* by Richard Wharfinger, seems to contain clues as to the origins of W.A.S.T.E. – in a dark welter of medieval European courier services and secret societies, 'an 800-year tradition of postal fraud'.

Either Oedipa Maas has stumbled on a *secret history of the world*, a huge and unsuspected story of interlocking destinies, or she has been deliberately duped by her eccentric dead lover, Pierce Inverarity. Or possibly she is insane, suffering from paranoid delusions. She turns for reassurance to her psychoanalyst, Dr Hilarius, only to find that he has cracked under the weight of his guilty Nazi past. In the novel's funniest scene, Oedipa tries to reason with the mad face-pulling doctor, who has locked himself in his office with a gun. Hilarius is convinced that he is about to be held to account for his work on 'experimentally-induced insanity' in Hitler's concentration camps – 'they had gone at their subjects with metronomes, serpents, Brechtian vignettes at midnight, surgical removal of certain glands, magic-lantern hallucinations, new drugs, threats recited over hidden loudspeakers, hypnotism, clocks that ran backward, and faces. Hilarius had been put in charge of faces.'

Clearly Dr Hilarius has fallen victim to his own techniques, but the reader is left uncertain as to the truth of Oedipa's situation. *The Crying of Lot 49* is a densely packed fantasia, alternately satirical and meditative, on the themes of reality, illusion and uncertainty. It is strewn with scientific metaphors, mock historiography, allusions to pop culture and references to Californian fads of the 1960s. It is a novel very much of its time and place, and self-evidently the work of a young writer, but it still succeeds in weaving its crazy hallucinogenic magic.

First edition: New York: Lippincott, 1966 (hardcover)
First British edition: London, Cape, 1967 (hardcover)
Most recent editions: New York, Harper & Row, and
London, Picador (paperbacks)

32

THOMAS BURNETT SWANN

Day of the Minotaur

'My history belongs to the princess Thea, niece of the great king Minos, and to her brother Icarus, named for the ill-fated son of Daedalus who drowned in the sea when his glider lost its wings.' This light and charming historical fantasy by a talented American author was first serialized in 1964 in a British magazine, *Science Fantasy*, under the title 'The Blue Monkeys'. The setting is Crete, *c.* 1500 BC, when the rough Achaeans of mainland Greece are beginning to harry the island's Minoan civilization. The central characters are two teenage children, Thea and Icarus – and their seven-foot friend, Eunostos the Minotaur. As the Achaeans attack, the prince and princess escape from their father's mansion, just south of Knossos, aboard one of the gliders built by the artificer Daedalus. They crash-land in the fabled Country of the Beasts, a little-known wooded area on the south of the island.

They hope to find protection in the forest, for these young people are themselves half-'beast', with violet eyes and pointed ears and hair of a greenish hue. Their mother was a Dryad from the Country of the Beasts, and she has passed her delicate beauty on to Thea: 'Fresh and flower-like she looked, with the careful cultivation of a garden in a palace courtyard, rather than the wildness of a meadow or a forest; soft as the petals of a crocus, slender as the stem of a tall Egyptian lotus. But the green-flecked brown of her hair and the bronze of her skin resembled no flower in any earthly garden. Perhaps in the Lower World, where the

Griffin Judge presides on his onyx throne, there are gardens with flowers like Thea.'

Sure enough, they are welcomed into the enchanted realm of the forest by its motley inhabitants – Centaurs, Dryads, Telchines, Panisci, blue monkeys and others. The benign leader of these woodland folk is the Minotaur, who also turns out to be the narrator of this whole story (he immediately falls in love with Thea). This is Arcadia with a cosy, Walt Disney touch. Eunostos the Minotaur lives beneath a dead tree-trunk:

> The house had once been a mountainous oak, broad as the Ring of the Bulls at Knossos . . . I had hollowed the trunk of my tree to encompass a garden, which held a folding chair of citrus wood, a clay oven for bread and honey cakes, a grill for roasting meat, and a fountain of hot spring water which served as my bath and also to wash my dishes . . . We descended a wooden staircase which coiled below the garden like the winding heart of a conch shell and opened abruptly into my den . . . The walls of the den were roots, twisted and smoothed into shape; and sturdier roots, resembling gnarled pillars, divided the room into separate nooks or dells.

But these over-sweet, children's-story qualities are offset by a playful sexiness (young Icarus dallies with Zoe the Dryad among others), and by an underlying sombreness of theme. The novel is about the war between cruel men and the unfallen Beasts: in its sentimental way, it deals with the rape of nature – a story which has no end. Before his untimely death, Thomas Burnett Swann (1928–76) went on to write a number of other engaging fantasies set in the worlds of Graeco-Roman myth. These include *The Weirwoods* (1967), *The Dolphin and the Deep* (1968) and *Green Phoenix* (1972). They all have much in common, but *The Forest of Forever* (1971) is the only one which is a direct sequel to *Day of the Minotaur*.

First edition: New York, Ace, 1966 (paperback)
First British edition: London, Granada, 1975 (paperback)

33

JACK VANCE

The Eyes of the Overworld

'On the heights above the river Xzan, at the site of certain ancient ruins, Iucounu the Laughing Magician had built a manse to his private taste: an eccentric structure of steep gables, balconies, sky-walks, cupolas, together with three spiral green glass towers through which the red sunlight shone in twisted glints and peculiar colours . . .' We are back in the world of *The Dying Earth* (*11*), where a swollen and enfeebled sun casts its rays over a fantastic landscape inhabited by misshapen creatures, dangerous men and malicious sorcerers. This is the long-delayed sequel to Jack Vance's masterpiece of 1950. It is a somewhat lighter, more humorous work, and, although episodic, it is more of a novel.

Vance's trickster hero is called Cugel the Clever – 'a man of many capabilities, with a disposition at once flexible and pertinacious. He was long of leg, deft of hand, light of finger, soft of tongue.' Cugel attempts to rob Iucounu the Laughing Magician, but is caught in a sorcerous trap. As punishment, Iucounu threatens him with the Charm of Forlorn Encystment – 'which constricts the subject in a pore some forty-five miles below the surface of the earth' – but instead he attaches a small creature, 'all claws, prongs, barbs and hooks', to Cugel's liver, and sends the would-be thief out on a perilous quest which the latter cannot refuse as long as his liver is threatened with agony. Cugel's task is to find one of the jewel-like Eyes of the Overworld, miraculous devices which enable men to view a higher realm of existence. To this end, he is carried away by a huge bird which dumps him on a forlorn beach on the far side of the world. The ever-resourceful Cugel is not daunted. Buoyed up by thoughts of revenge, he soon succeeds in procuring the much-sought bauble; and after fighting, cheating and sweet-talking his way through numerous hair-raising adventures, he wends his long way home and delivers it to the ungrateful magician. Whereupon his plans for vengeance go awry and he finds himself banished once more. Cugel's stratagems are sometimes brutal, as are those of any legendary trickster, but the whole story is narrated with unfailing humour, inventiveness and verbal facility.

The Eyes of the Overworld is fine in its way, but it does not have the dying-fall beauty of Vance's first book (which combined low humour and vaulting imagination in a near-perfect blend). Nor do the much later volumes in which the author has again visited his 'Dying Earth' setting – *Cugel's Saga* (1983) and *Rhialto the Marvellous* (1984) – quite succeed in recapturing the magic of the original. Nevertheless the four books add up to one of the most impressive and influential achievements in the field of 'science fantasy'. Vance's work has left its mark on writers as various and talented as Michael Moorcock, M. John Harrison and Gene Wolfe (not to mention Michael Shea, an unashamed emulator – see the entry for his *Nifft the Lean* [79]). Other notable fantasies by Jack Vance include his ongoing 'Lyonesse' series, of which the first two volumes are *Suldrun's Garden* (1983) and *The Green Pearl* (1985). These are big novels which present us with a most unusual slant on the Matter of Britain. Although he has been writing for decades, it is still too early to make a full assessment of Vance's contribution to modern fantasy. But clearly he is one of the genre's major authors.

First edition: New York, Ace, 1966 (paperback)
First British edition: London, Granada, 1972 (paperback)
Most recent editions: New York, Baen, and London, Grafton (paperbacks)

34

ALAN GARNER

The Owl Service

During the 1960s Alan Garner rapidly became Britain's most renowned writer of books for children. He began with *The Weirdstone of Brisingamen* (1960) and *The Moon of Gomrath* (1963), a pair of splendidly-titled fantasies about a young brother and sister who have magical adventures in a legend-haunted district of Cheshire. These were followed by *Elidor* (1965), a tale of the supernatural set in Manchester; and by *The Owl Service*, another extremely effective blend of mythic fantasy and contemporary realism. At first glance, the latter may be taken for a children's 'holiday adventure story' (a genre made popular by Arthur Ransome and Enid Blyton), but one does not have to read far to realize that it is a novel of rare imaginative power – an astonishingly sensitive and subtle fantasy.

The setting is a valley in Wales. Alison and Roger are English teenagers, holidaying with the former's mother and the latter's father (who have recently married). Their Welsh housekeeper has a son, Gwyn, a clever grammar-school boy of about their own age. The three adolescents become friends, and share the excitement of exploring the old stone house and its environs. They hear mysterious scratching sounds in the loft, but all they discover there is a dusty old dinner service. Gwyn brings the plates down, and Alison copies the floral patterns on them, folding her drawings to make paper owls. It becomes an alarming obsession, and as she makes the model owls the original patterns disappear from the plates. Meanwhile some plaster falls from a wall in the billiard room, to reveal the portrait of a beautiful maiden surrounded by flowers.

A supernatural power has been let loose in the valley, something centuries old which had been temporarily trapped in patterns of flowers and owls. Tensions grow between the three young people: rivalries which spring from sexual jealousy and class prejudice. Without realizing it at first, they are re-enacting a Welsh legend from *The Mabinogion* – the story of Blodeuwedd the flower-maiden whose faithlessness led to the deaths of two men. Also caught up in the mysterious events are Gwyn's superstitious mother and the apparently half-witted gardener known as Huw Halfbacon. It gradually becomes plain that the previous generation was involved in a similar pattern of love and tragedy, and that these events will recur for ever unless the cycle can be broken by an 'outsider' with sufficient force of personality.

Garner is a superbly economical writer: descriptive and discursive passages are kept to a minimum, and most of the novel consists of dialogue. The voices are well caught, with convincing Welsh cadences in the speech of Gwyn and his 'Mam' (and a mystical lyricism in the case of Huw Halfbacon). The characterizations are exceedingly sharp: not only the three adolescents, but the four principal adults are very well drawn – even though one of them, Alison's mother, never appears on stage. With its emphasis on ancient Celtic legend, *The Owl Service* could be described as a British Western, wherein the Welsh characters are the redskinned 'natives' – primitive, tragic, poetically wise. But at the same time it is a realistic tale of modern teenagers' passions and frustrations.

Like C. S. Lewis before him, Alan Garner (born 1934) was to become a dominant force in the field of fantasy for younger readers. A small school of British writers took their inspiration from his early books. Perhaps the most notable of these is Susan Cooper, whose five-volume sequence of novels known collectively as *The Dark is Rising*

(1965–77) is regarded by many readers as one of the best of juvenile fantasies.

> *First edition*: London, Collins, 1967 (hardcover)
> *First American edition*: New York, Collins, 1979 (hardcover)
> *Most recent edition*: London, Fontana (paperback)

35

IRA LEVIN

Rosemary's Baby

This sly, seductive, impeccably-written horror novel was a huge commercial success. Levin's frightening little book, and the Roman Polanski film which followed a year later ('the single most faithful adaptation of a novel ever to come out of Hollywood,' in Levin's own words), triggered the whole modern boom in American horror fiction – making possible the success of William Peter Blatty's (much inferior) *The Exorcist* (1971), the *Omen/Damien* cycle of films, and the careers of novelists Stephen King and Peter Straub among many others. (Alas for Fritz Leiber, his somewhat similar *Conjure Wife* [13] had been well ahead of its time.)

Rosemary Woodhouse is a happily married young woman living in New York. Her handsome and charming husband, Guy, is an actor who makes his living from TV commercials and bit-parts in plays. They move into a much sought-after apartment in the Bramford Building – 'old, black, and elephantine . . . a warren of high-ceilinged apartments prized for their fireplaces and Victorian detail' – where they soon make the acquaintance of a neighbouring couple, Roman and Minnie Castavet. 'His wide, thin-lipped mouth was rosy pink, as if lipsticked; his cheeks were chalky, his eyes small and bright in deep sockets. She was big-nosed, with a sullen fleshy underlip. She wore pink-rimmed eyeglasses on a neckchain that dipped down from behind plain pearl earrings.' The Castevets are a good deal older than Rosemary and Guy, and at first Rosemary finds them eccentric and faintly disturbing. However, Guy takes to them warmly, spending long hours in their apartment discussing theatrical matters.

Rosemary becomes broody, and generally dissatisfied with her life. However, the selfish Guy's career is blossoming: he gains a leading stage role when a rival actor is mysteriously blinded. All of a sudden, he is solicitous towards his young wife: 'I've been so busy tearing my hair out over *my* career that I haven't given Thought One to yours. Let's have a baby, okay?' It is Rosemary's dearest wish, and she begins to prepare herself for motherhood. She is happy, even if the smelly good-luck charm ('tannis root') and the strange foodstuffs and drinks which Minnie Castevet presses upon her become a source of increasing irritation. And one night she has an extremely unpleasant dream: 'She opened her eyes and looked into yellow furnace-eyes, smelled sulphur and tannis root, felt wet breath on her mouth, heard lust-grunts and the breathing of onlookers . . .'

Poor Rosemary's pregnancy takes a horrifying course, and its result is monstrous. Little by little, she finds out what is really happening, and attempts to rebel against the part she has been forced to play. Clues to the occult nature of the events are strewn carefully throughout the novel, building a strong atmosphere of unease. It is an expertly constructed story, a playwright's book, in which every physical detail and every line of dialogue counts. Ira Levin (born 1929) was a successful writer for the stage and television before he published *Rosemary's Baby* (a 1965 musical called *Drat! The Cat!*, referred to in the novel, was in fact his work) and his ability to spin a cunning plot stood him in good stead when he came to write this best-seller. But the main reason for the novel's appeal lies in the characterization of Rosemary. She is a modern American Everywoman, a sweetly good-natured middle-class girl with whom most readers can identify – and she is simultaneously the persecuted maiden of the old Gothic novels, a prey to unfeeling men, grotesque old biddies, and an all-too male Devil.

First edition: New York, Random House, 1967 (hardcover)
First British edition: London, Michael Joseph, 1967
(hardcover)
Most recent editions: New York, Dell, and London, Pan
(paperbacks)

36

FLANN O'BRIEN

The Third Policeman

This odd, nightmarish book was first published a year after its author's death. Brian O'Nolan (1911–66) was a well-loved Irish journalist who wrote several novels under his 'Flann O'Brien' pseudonym, the best-known being his first, the comic *At Swim-Two-Birds* (1939). *The Third Policeman* was written shortly after that near-masterpiece, but lay unpublished for several decades. Despite this long neglect, it proved to be a unique fantasy, both frightening and whimsical. The story unfolds in breezy, deadpan style, and it begins with a murder. The narrator (who cannot remember his own name) recounts how he and his friend, the 'lazy and idle-minded' John Divney, slay an old man for his money:

> I went forward mechanically, swung the spade over my shoulder and smashed the blade of it with all my strength against the protruding chin. I felt and almost heard the fabric of his skull crumple up crisply like an eggshell. I do not know how often I struck him after that but I did not stop until I was tired.
>
> I threw the spade down and looked around for Divney. He was nowhere to be seen . . . My heart stumbled painfully in its beating. A chill of fright ran right through me. If anybody should come, nothing in the world would save me from the gallows . . .

A worse fate than the gallows is in store for him. He has of course been double-crossed by his accomplice, who has rushed off to secure their victim's treasure.

Later, the narrator visits the old man's apparently deserted house, in search of the money-box. He hears a cough, and turns around to see the old man himself sitting at a table and drinking tea: 'His face was terrifying but his eyes in the middle of it had a quality of chill and horror which made his other features look to me almost friendly. The skin was like faded parchment with an arrangement of puckers and wrinkles which created between them an expression of fathomless inscrutability.' Our protagonist does not realize it at this point (and nor does the reader), but he has in fact died and entered the afterlife – murdered, in his turn, by the treacherous Divney. It transpires that the narrator has been damned by his own monstrous act, and is now doomed to wander an increasingly surreal Irish landscape on his hunt for the missing money-box.

Scattered throughout the novel are copious citations (with footnotes) of a lunatic philosopher called de Selby. These provide much of the novel's high comedy. The narrator was at work on a 'de Selby Codex' at the time he was seduced into committing the murder – he had hoped the ill-gotten cash would help pay for the book's publication. Now the spirit of de Selby returns to haunt him, in the persons of two officers he encounters at a country police station. These mad policemen, one of whom has an unhealthy obsession with bicycles, vex the narrator with their brain-teasing conundrums. They show him various enigmatic toys, including a set of Chinese boxes, the smallest of which cannot be seen even with the help of a powerful magnifying glass ('Such work must be very hard on the eyes,' says the hero drily). Boxes within boxes, infinite regression, cyclical experiences – gradually the narrator realizes that he is eking out his existence in a peculiar kind of hell. All is confirmed when he meets the mysterious third policeman, and finds himself beginning to relive the entire cycle of events since his death.

First edition: London, MacGibbon & Kee, 1967 (hardcover)
Most recent edition: London, Grafton (paperback)

37

ANDREW SINCLAIR

Gog

A most unusual English novel, this. Although very British in its subject-matter, *Gog* was the most thoroughgoing attempt of the 1960s to write a large 'mythological' metafiction in the contemporary American style. In this wildly imaginative book Andrew Sinclair (born 1935) reveals that he has more in common with, say, John Barth or Thomas Pynchon than he has with any of his compatriots. Perhaps this is not unconnected with the fact that the energetic Mr Sinclair was partially educated at Harvard and Columbia universities (following a conventional, if privileged, English education at Eton and Cambridge) and has also written several non-fiction books on American topics. In addition to his non-fiction and film-making activities, he is the author of many novels, of which *Gog* is certainly the most ambitious. Sadly, it seems to have sunk like a stone, and is now a neglected work – despite high praise from some critics at the time of its first publication.

It is 1945, in the period between the German surrender and the final defeat of Japan. The bewildered hero, a historian named Dr George Griffin, has lost his memory and imagines that he is 'Gog' (the erstwhile subject of his 'great research project, the History of Gog and Magog from the Beginning of Albion to the End of England'). A big man, nearly seven feet tall, he is discovered lying on a beach near Edinburgh, and it is assumed that he is a survivor from a torpedoed ship. His only distinguishing marks are the tattooed 'Gog' and 'Magog' on his fists.

These are the names of the legendary giants who were taken captive by Brutus, the refugee Trojan who is supposed to have become the first king of Britain. According to the medieval story, the twin giants were set to work as palace porters in London (or Troy-Novant, as it was originally called), and afterwards their statues stood at the city's Guildhall for many centuries. The tale is worked into the fabric of Sinclair's novel, along with countless other references to British history, legend and lore – from Wayland Smith through Boadicea to Robin Hood and William Blake's 'prophetic books'.

Griffin-alias-Gog escapes from hospital, steals some clothes and bread, and sets out on a long tramp towards London. Maurice, a Cockney spiv whom he meets in an Edinburgh pub, tells him that the people now rule in the nation's capital (for this is shortly after the Labour Party's victory in the general election) – and Gog develops a confused desire to witness this political marvel for himself. He is certain of one thing, namely that he is 'a fool for freedom', on the common people's side in the struggle against the powers that be. As he walks through southern Scotland and northern England, he meets many enemies of freedom, all of whom have names beginning with 'M' and are associated with his evil brother, Magog. But he also meets the Bagman, a lunatic revolutionary whose dearest wish is to commandeer the airwaves; and a Welsh schoolmaster, Evans the Latin, who believes that the Celtic peoples of Britain should rise up against their 'Limey' masters. And as he travels 'down the little lanes that vein the face of England', he experiences many fantastic adventures (or delusions) which seem to recapitulate the history of the land. His memories gradually return to him, as he is beaten and buffeted from one horrific or ludicrous episode to the next, until finally he finds himself hoisted in triumph on to the shoulders of the London folk – those 'cockneys and costers and hawkers and buskers, skivvies and floozies and chippies and chars'. *Gog* is a brilliant fantasy-travelogue, lyrically rendered in a high comic style which is made all the richer by its wealth of mythological allusions.

First edition: London, Weidenfeld & Nicholson, 1967 (hardcover)
Most recent edition: Harmondsworth, Penguin (paperback)

38

PETER S. BEAGLE

The Last Unicorn

'The unicorn lived in a lilac wood, and she lived all alone. She was very old, though she did not know it, and she was no longer the careless colour of sea foam, but rather the colour of snow falling on a moonlit night. But her eyes were still clear and unwearied, and she still moved like a shadow on the sea.' So begins this fairy-tale novel which has enchanted many readers and gained something of a cult following. Apparently simple and almost child-like in its narrative line, it is written in a limpid prose which succeeds in expressing adult complexities. And like Beagle's *A Fine and Private Place* (*24*), it contains a good deal of gentle humour. It tells how the last unicorn sets out from her wood in search of others of her kind – a seemingly hopeless quest, for she finds a sadly fallen world, one whose inhabitants no longer have eyes for the marvellous. Most people 'see' her as some sort of peculiar horse.

A few folk recognize her true nature, however. One is the witch-like proprietor of Mommy Fortuna's Midnight Carnival, a dismal travelling circus whose advertising slogan is '*creatures of night, brought to light*'. Mommy Fortuna's cages contain a motley collection of forlorn animals – a lion, a crocodile, a mangy dog, an ape, a boa constrictor and others – but when viewed from a certain angle these poor beasts take on the appearance of a scorpion-tailed manticore, a fiery dragon, Cerberus the three-headed dog, and the Midgard Serpent. (The reader is reminded slightly of Charles G. Finney's odd little fantasy novel *The Circus of Dr Lao*, 1935.) For a while the unicorn is trapped behind

111

the iron bars of a carnival cage, but she soon escapes from there with the help of a new-found friend, Schmendrick the Magician: 'So they fled across the night together, step by step, the tall man in black and the horned white beast. The magician crept as close to the unicorn's light as he dared, for beyond it moved hungry shadows . . .'

Schmendrick is a bumbling and accident-prone master of the magical arts ('I must have gotten the accent wrong,' he says when one of his spells fails to work), but he proves to be a loyal companion for the unicorn in her search for the land of King Haggard – where she has been told that some of her 'people' may still be living. The unlikely pair are joined on their picaresque quest by Molly Grue, a rough outlaw who proves to have a heart of gold. 'Unicorns are for beginnings,' complains the jealous Schmendrick, 'for innocence and purity, for newness . . . for young girls.' In other words, unicorns are for virgins, but: 'Molly was stroking the unicorn's throat as timidly as though she were blind. She dried her grimy tears on the white mane. "You don't know much about unicorns," she said.' Under the beautiful creature's influence Molly seems to grow younger and more carefree. Eventually the travellers arrive in King Haggard's realm, and this turns out to be a blighted wasteland which the unicorn and her friends will help to redeem. The last unicorn fights a great red bull, and drives it into the sea – thus releasing all her one-horned kinsfolk, who return to their wooded glades deep in the reawakened land.

Despite the commercial success of this joyous fable, Peter S. Beagle has written few works of fiction. His later stories in a fantastic vein are *Lila the Werewolf* (1974), a slim novella, and *The Folk of the Air* (1986), a full-length novel. Nevertheless he is one of the most influential modern writers of fantasy: along with Ursula Le Guin (see the following entry), he helped to consolidate the genre – and to open the way for the great fantasy boom which became so vital a part of the American publishing scene during the 1970s.

First edition: New York, Viking, 1968 (hardcover)
First British edition: London, The Bodley Head, 1968 (hardcover)
Most recent editions: New York, Del Rey, and London, Unwin (paperbacks)

39

URSULA K. LE GUIN

A Wizard of Earthsea

Earthsea is a world of islands surrounded by endless ocean, and here young Ged, a prentice wizard, grows to maturity. His mother is long dead, but his aunt, a village witch, teaches him how to control the beasts of the field and the birds of the sky. He gains the use-name 'Sparrowhawk', for in this world of magic one's true name should be kept secret: a knowledge of names is the key to the magician's art. At the age of thirteen Ged goes to live with the mage Ogion. The latter senses great power in the boy – already Ged has managed to defend his village against a murderous band of raiders by magically manipulating the weather – and he knows that one day this callow lad will grow to be a mighty wizard. But old Ogion does not force the pace, for Ged must learn patience as the beginning of true wisdom:

> Still no marvels and enchantments occurred. All winter there was nothing but the heavy pages of the Runebook turning, and the rain and the snow falling; and Ogion would come in from roaming the icy forests or from looking after his goats, and stamp the snow off his boots, and sit down in silence by the fire. And the mage's long, listening silence would fill the room, and fill Ged's mind, until sometimes it seemed he had forgotten what words sounded like: and when Ogion spoke at last it was as if he had, just then and for the first time, invented speech . . .
>
> As the spring came on, quick and bright, Ogion often

sent Ged forth to gather herbs on the meadows above Re
Albi, and told him to take as long as he liked about it,
giving him freedom to spend all day wandering by
rainfilled streams and through the woods and over wet
green fields in the sun. Ged went with delight each time,
and stayed out till night; but he did not entirely forget
the herbs.

In time, he goes to study at the school for wizards on the
magical isle of Roke. There he proves to be an extremely
apt pupil, but he suffers a fall from grace when he foolishly
engages in a jealous contest with another student. An evil
entity, a shadow or *gebbeth*, is released into the world by
Ged's intemperate dabbling in forces he cannot yet control.
The boy comes close to death, but he is nursed back to
health by the wise masters of Roke – and eventually goes
out to earn his living as a workaday wizard. As he wanders
the multitudinous islands of Earthsea, he tames dragons
and overcomes other ancient perils, but at all times he is
haunted by the evil shadow which is his unique responsibil-
ity and spiritual burden. At length he learns how to
confront the *gebbeth*: he comes to know its name, and is
able to rid the world of his shadow by absorbing it into
himself.

This is a beautiful story – poetic, thrilling and profound.
Although it deals in otherwordly magic, it has a serene
consistency: the supernatural details are logically (and wittily) developed, and indeed the whole book is founded on a
bedrock of anthropological and psychological 'realism'. Of
all the fantasy novels for younger readers since World War
II, *A Wizard of Earthsea* is the masterpiece. Ursula Le Guin
(born 1929) is a finer writer than C. S. Lewis, more lucid
than Alan Garner, more original than Susan Cooper or Joy
Chant, and more fluent than any of her own American
imitators. In addition to her highly-praised science fiction
novels, she has produced two more books set in the world
of Earthsea: *The Tombs of Atuan* (1971) and *The Farthest*

Shore (1973). These are quite separate novels, although Ged appears in both.

> *First edition*: Berkeley, Parnassus Press, 1968 (hardcover)
> *First British edition*: London, Gollancz, 1971 (hardcover)
> *Most recent editions*: Harmondsworth, Penguin, and New York, Bantam (paperbacks; also available in omnibus volumes entitled *The Earthsea Trilogy*)

40

FRITZ LEIBER

The Swords of Lankhmar

Robert E. Howard invented the form, but Fritz Leiber is
credited with coining the descriptive label: 'swords and
sorcery'. Leiber began writing his good-humoured, roister-
ing tales of the barbarian Fafhrd and the sneak-thief known
as the Gray Mouser in the late 1930s, shortly after Howard's
death – though the first volume of the heroes' exploits,
Two Sought Adventure, did not appear until 1957 (it was
later expanded and retitled *Swords Against Death*). Since
then there have been five more books in the 'Swords' series,
but only one of them, *The Swords of Lankhmar*, counts as a
full-length novel. 'Fafhrd and the Mouser are rogues
through and through,' says Leiber in his preface to the
book, 'though each has in him a lot of humanity and at
least a diamond chip of the spirit of true adventure. They
drink, they feast, they wench, they brawl, they steal, they
gamble . . . It strikes me that Fafhrd and the Gray Mouser
are almost at the opposite extreme from the heroes of
Tolkien. My stuff is at least equally as fantastic as his, but
it's an earthier sort of fantasy . . .' This is true. One of the
elements which makes Leiber's fiction so different from
Tolkien's (and Howard's) is its erotic spiciness. There is a
great deal of nudity and sexual dalliance in the imaginary
world of Nehwon – but there is also much repartee, magic
and violent action. And everything is narrated in a rich
descriptive prose.

In this novel, the city of Lankhmar is suffering from a
plague of rats. Fafhrd and the Gray Mouser are commissioned by the dissolute overlord Glipkerio to guard a grain-

ship which bears gifts to another town. They are almost overcome by a rebellion of the rats aboard their vessel, before a two-headed sea-monster inadvertently comes to their rescue. Back in the city once more, after successfully completing the sea voyage, they find that the rodent-plague has taken a firmer hold:

> The rats were looting by night in Lankhmar. Everywhere in the age-old city they were pilfering, and not only food. They filched the greenish bent brass coins off a dead carter's eyes and the platinum-set nose, ear, and lip jewels from the triply locked gem chest of Glipkerio's wraith-thin aunt, gnawing in the thick oak a postern door neat as a fairy tale. The wealthiest grocer lost all his husked Hrusp nuts, gray caviar from sea-sundered Ool Plerns, dried lark's hearts, strength-imparting tiger meal, sugar-dusted ghostfingers, and ambrosia wafers, while less costly dainties were untouched. Rare parchments were taken from the Great Library . . . Sweetmeats vanished from bedside tables, toys from princes' nurseries, tidbits from gold inlaid silver appetizer trays, and flinty grain from horses' feedbags. Bracelets were unhooked from the wrists of embracing lovers, the pouches and snugly-flapped pockets of crossbow-armed rat watchers were picked, and from under the noses of cats and ferrets their food was stolen.
>
> The most cunning traps were set, subtle poisons laid out invitingly, ratholes stoppered with leaden plugs and brazen plates, candles lit in dark corners, unwinking watch kept in every likely spot. All to no avail.

Much worse is to come, before our ingenious heroes are able to defeat the gruesome curse. They have to call on sorcerous help from Sheelba of the Eyeless Face and Ningauble the Seven-Eyed Wizard; the Mouser must shrink in size, and descend into the rat's underground maze; and Fafhrd must learn how to unleash the dreaded War Cats.

The tale builds to a thoroughly satisfactory climax, and it is wonderful, extravagant fun all the way.

First edition: New York, Ace, 1968 (paperback)
First British edition: London, Hart-Davis, 1969 (hardcover)
Most recent editions: New York, Ace, and London, Grafton (paperbacks)

41

JAMES BLISH

Black Easter and *The Day After Judgment*

In recent decades there have been many novels about black magic – Dennis Wheatley was one popular author who spun them out like yard-goods – but few can have been as scrupulously researched, or as drily convincing, as this two-part work by the American science fiction writer James Blish (1921–75). As the author states in a preface to the first volume: 'its background is based as closely as possible upon the writings and actual working manuals of practising magicians working in the Christian tradition from the thirteenth to the eighteenth centuries, from the *Ars Magna* of Ramon Lull, through the various *Keys* of pseudo-Solomon, pseudo-Agrippa, pseudo-Honorius and so on, to the grimoires themselves. All of the books mentioned in the text actually exist . . .' Blish treats medieval magic as though it were an exact science or a workable technology, a body of knowledge as effective as modern physics and engineering.

These two slim novels do constitute one work, though Blish did not give it an overall title. The first (and superior) half is called *Black Easter, or Faust Aleph-Null*. The story's leading Faust-figure is a black magician named Theron Ware, US-born but living in Italy. Although primarily driven by a lust for knowledge, he performs the black arts in a businesslike way, selling his diabolical skills only to the very rich. One such client is Mr Baines, a munitions manufacturer who fears that the future of his bloody trade is threatened by the existence of nuclear weapons, and who hires Theron Ware's services in order to restore some chaos and carnage to an over-peaceful world. Ware explains that all acts of magic, without exception, depend on the control of demons. It is by invoking these fallen angels that he will be able to give Mr Baines what he desires. The two agree to do business, and they begin by plotting the deaths of a politician and a famous scientist. After these test-cases prove successful, Baines divulges his *real* wish – namely to loose all the demons of Hell on to the earth for one night.

There is little narrative flow to *Black Easter*, and the characterization is perfunctory (Brother Domenico Garelli, the token man of God, seems very much a supernumerary figure). The strengths of the story lie in the descriptive set-pieces, and in the definite chill which they evoke. At the climactic scene of the conjuration of demons, a 'Grand Circle' is drawn upon the floor of Theron Ware's labora-tory: 'The circle proper was made of strips of the sacrificial kid, with the hair still on it, fastened to the floor at the cardinal points with four nails that, Ware explained, had been drawn from the coffin of a child. On the northeast arc, under the word BERKAIAL, there rested on the strips the body of a male bat that had been drowned in blood; on the northeast, under the word AMASARAC, the skull of a parri-cide; on the southwest, under the word ASARADEL, the horns of a goat; and on the southwest, under the word ARIBECL, sat Ware's cat' (an obscenely fat beast which is fed only on the flesh of dead babies). These gruesome preparations bear fruit, and the denouement of this first novel is suitably horrid and awe-inspiring. The second volume, *The Day After Judgment*, seems a lesser work, descending occasionally into farce – though the image of the infernal city of Dis arising in Death Valley is certainly a memorable one.

First editions: New York, Doubleday, 1968 and 1971 (hardcovers)
First British editions: London, Faber, 1969 and 1972 (hardcovers)
Most recent editions: London, Sphere (paperback; the two novels in one volume), and New York, Avon (separate paperbacks)

42

The Green Man

Amis has a large reputation as a comic novelist, but this ingenious latter-day ghost story has been much underrated. Written with the author's customary acidulous wit, it is in part a comedy of manners (which mocks the shallow trendiness of certain aspects of English middle-class life in the late 1960s), in part a sex farce, and in part a moving study of failed communication between husband and wife, father and daughter. It is also an expertly constructed and highly atmospheric tale of supernatural horror.

In its opening pages, the first-person narrative puts one in mind of John Cleese's hilarious television series *Fawlty Towers* (to such an extent that I am convinced Cleese must have drawn his inspiration for the irascible hotelier Basil Fawlty and his dim-witted Spanish waiter, Manuel, from a few asides Amis makes in this novel). The narrator is Maurice Allington, 53-year-old proprietor of The Green Man, an inn which has stood in the Hertfordshire country-side since the Middle Ages. Maurice is an alcoholic, something of a lecher, and a thorough-going misanthrope. His exasperation is fuelled by his customers, his staff, and his family: 'As if in the service of some underground anti-hotelier organization, successive guests tried to rape the chambermaid, called for a priest at 3 A.M., wanted a room to take girlie photographs in, were found dead in bed . . . After a year of no worse than average conduct, the Spanish kitchen porter went into a heavy bout of Peeping Tom behaviour, notably but not at all exclusively at the grille outside the ladies' lavatory . . . The deep-fat fryer caught fire twice, once during a session of the South Hertfordshire branch of the Wine and Food Society. My wife seemed lethargic, my daughter withdrawn. My father, now in his eightieth year, had another stroke . . .'

On top of all this, Maurice is drinking too much whisky and suffering from hypnagogic hallucinations at night. As an antidote, he hopes to lure his doctor's blonde wife to bed – preferably when his own attractive young wife is there to share the experience (this act of troilism does eventually take place, and it is a sore disappointment to him). The inn has a reputation for being haunted, but Maurice regards this as useful bait for credulous tourists: in his seven years as proprietor he has seen no supernatural manifestations, nor is he inclined to believe in such things. However, an uncanny dimension begins to unfold as early as the third page of the novel, when the narrator encounters a pale young woman in old-fashioned dress who is standing at the stairhead outside his room. She vanishes when Maurice's attention is distracted momentarily, and at first neither he nor the reader is aware that she is a ghost. But events become progressively more sinister after Maurice's aged father dies, in the middle of a dinner party, with a look of fearful surprise on his face . . .

Amis deploys his supernatural machinery brilliantly: old documents, the ghost of a seventeenth-century child-killer, a midnight disinterment, even a face-to-face conversation with God. All this alternates with passages of comedy and satire, but is none the less chilling. The long-awaited Green Man himself – a creature sprung from the trees whose face consists of 'smooth dusty bark like the trunk of a Scotch pine, with irregular eye-sockets in which a fungoid luminescence glimmered, and a wide grinning mouth that showed more than a dozen teeth made of jagged stumps of rotting wood' – is a truly nightmarish monster. Kingsley Amis (born 1922) has written several genre 'entertainments' (a James Bond thriller, a pastiche detective novel, and so on) in addition to his more avowedly serious novels. *The*

Green Man surpasses these, and deserves to be considered as one of its author's finest works.

First edition: London, Cape, 1969 (hardcover)
Most recent edition: London, Granada (paperback)

43

AVRAM DAVIDSON

The Phoenix and the Mirror or, The Enigmatic Speculum

Avram Davidson (born 1923) is one of the oddball writers
of the American fantasy field. A past editor of *The Magazine
of Fantasy and Science Fiction*, he has written paperback-
original novels with such off-putting titles as *Clash of Star-
Kings* (1966) and *Ursus of Ultima Thule* (1973). Yet Davidson, like his late friend James Blish, is an erudite author
who draws his inspiration from obscure byways of historical knowledge. *The Phoenix and the Mirror* carries an
author's note which explains the story's provenance:

'During the Middle Ages a copious group of legends
became associated with the name of Vergil, attributing
to the author of *The Aeneid* all manner of heroic, scientific
and magical powers – to such an extent, indeed, that
most of the world . . . looked upon him as a nigroman-
cer, or sorcerer. From the Dark Ages to the Renascence,
the popular view of the ancient world as reflected in the
Vergilean Legends was far from the historical and actual
. . . It is a world of never-never, and yet it is a world
true to its own curious lights – a backward projection of
medievalism, an awed and confused transmogrification
of quasi-forgotten ancient science . . . Such is the setting
of the novel *The Phoenix and the Mirror*. It is projected as
part of a series, the entire corpus to be known as *Vergil
Magus*.

The story tells how Vergil, an eminent citizen of Naples,
is commissioned against his will by the beautiful Queen

Cornelia to construct a 'virgin speculum' – a magical bronze mirror which has never reflected a face. The queen wants this device in order to locate her missing daughter (although she has other, hidden, motives). She coerces Vergil by seducing him and stealing part of his soul. The Magus has no choice but to set about the nigh-impossible task of manufacturing the bronze speculum. He must obtain quantities of freshly-mined tin and copper ore – no easy matter. He sends birds to fabled Tinland (presumably Britain) to fetch the first of these ores: 'They would see sights, as they veered and circled, that no man ever saw: the sun rising from the sea beneath them, like a disc of burnished brass; beneath them, too, the icy alps; the Great Forest, stretching farther than the knowledge of man; and, at length, after many days and many perils, the storm-buffeted air and water of the cold, grey Northern Sea . . .'

While these avian emissaries are procuring the tin, Vergil sets out on a hazardous voyage to the east – to Cyprus, island of copper. The way is barred by brutal Hunnish pirates, but Vergil is able to win passage by playing off one of their hereditary kings against the others. The shore-camp of these dreadful Huns is wittily described: 'A stench of night-soil and stale urine and rotten fish, of ill-cured hides, dried sweat, old dogs, unwashed clothes, sour mares' milk, and other elements defying analysis hung over the camp. The Sea-Huns were said to bathe but once a year . . . and on that day, it was told, the fish in all the circumjacent seas died in great multitudes.' Vergil's adventures on Cyprus prove to be equally memorable; and the detailed description of the actual making of the speculum, on his return to Naples, is a *tour de force*. The flurry of action at the end – when Vergil travels to Africa for a showdown with the Phoenix, the legendary bird of fire – seems a little rushed, but overall the novel is an eccentric masterpiece: highly original in its evocation of a 'Medieval' Roman Empire, and impressively learned in its vocabulary. It is a pity that Davidson has not been able to summon the energy to complete his projected *Vergil Magus* sequence. Just one further novel has appeared, after an eighteen-year gap: *Vergil in Averno* (1987).

First edition: New York, Doubleday, 1969 (hardcover)
First British edition: London, Granada, 1975 (paperback)
Most recent edition: New York, Ace (paperback)

44

PHILIP JOSÉ FARMER

A Feast Unknown

Philip José Farmer (born 1918) has a name as a science fiction writer, though much of his sf has a fantasy 'feel' to it. He has long been obsessed by superheroes, particularly the pulp-magazine variety fondly remembered from his own boyhood reading, and in this outrageous novel he brings together two of the greatest – Tarzan of the Apes, Lord of the Jungle, and Doc Savage, the Man of Bronze. Here they are disguised as 'Lord Grandrith' and 'Doc Caliban', and in fact the jokey subtitle of the novel is 'Volume IX of *The Memoirs of Lord Grandrith* edited by Philip José Farmer.' Grandrith is clearly Edgar Rice Burroughs's Tarzan (or Lord Greystoke): born in 1888, son of an aristocratic English couple marooned on the West African coast, and raised by a relict tribe of pre-human hominids ('great apes') known as the Folk. At the beginning of the book he is seventy-nine years old but looks and feels thirty. In this wicked and apocryphal addition to the Tarzan saga, the hero is endowed with perpetual youth (both he and Doc Caliban are unwilling servants of 'the Nine', a secret society of immortals who possess an elixir of life). He is also endowed with great sexual potency.

A Feast Unknown was written for a series of porno-graphic novels issued by a fly-by-night Californian publisher in the late 1960s. It has a strong sexual (and specifically sado-masochistic) content which many readers may find repugnant. Certainly, it is unsuitable for children. However, it is not merely a sick and exploitative exercise in 'talking dirty': it is written with a verve and imaginative force which have kept the book alive. At times it is very funny, but it can be seen to have a serious purpose. Farmer is intent on bringing into the daylight many of the hidden, unconscious fantasies which underlie all superhero adventure stories. He is saying that violence is often rooted in sexuality, and that the vicarious violence of escapist fiction appeals in a perverse way to the sexual instincts of its readers. We may not wish to be told such truths, but it is hard for us to gainsay them.

It is a fast-moving first-person narrative, told by Lord Grandrith. As a result of various misunderstandings, Grandrith and Doc Caliban are enemies throughout most of the novel. Both are suffering from a sexual dysfunction which has presumably been caused by the foul elixir administered by the Nine: each of them is horrified to discover that his every act of violence is accompanied by an involuntary orgasm. At one point Grandrith kills a lion, in a replay of a standard set-piece scene from the Burroughs novels and the Johnny Weissmuller films – but this time there is a difference: 'As I felt the neck muscles weaken . . . and my arm muscles gain in strength . . . I became conscious of an approaching orgasm. I don't know when my penis had swelled and my testicles gathered themselves for the explosion. But my penis was jammed between the lion's back and my belly, and it was throbbing and beginning to jerk . . . At that moment, the lion's neck gave way. As the muscles loosened and the bones broke, I spurted, sliming the fur and my belly.' After the kill, Grandrith swallows some of the lion's sperm, enjoying 'the heavy big-feline taste and odour of it'. Similar actions and reactions are described when the two heroes first meet and grapple with each other outside the caves of the Nine. Their rivalry is intensely, nakedly sexual – and that candid element makes this book a fantasy-romance quite unlike any other in modern popular fiction.

First edition: North Hollywood, Essex House, 1969 (paperback)
First British edition: London, Quartet Books, 1975 (paperback)
Most recent editions: New York, Playboy Press, and London, Grafton (paperbacks)

45

R.A. LAFFERTY

Fourth Mansions

I described Avram Davidson as one of the American fantasy field's oddball writers. Even odder is Raphael Aloysius Lafferty (born 1914), who must rank as one of the most madcap writers of them all. Quite justly, his work has been described by one reviewer as 'profoundly dotty, and dottily profound'. His many novels and short stories are best read in an Irish accent, for they are whimsical tall tales, full of blarney and mysticism. Most of Lafferty's work is classifiable as science fiction (just about), although in a sense all of it is sheer fantasy. His best-known novel, *Past Master* (1968), is about the resurrection of Sir Thomas More on an alien planet some five hundred years hence. *Fourth Mansions*, while much of a muchness with the rest of Lafferty's *oeuvre*, has fewer of the trappings of sf and fits the 'fantasy' label more comfortably.

I should attempt to explain that faintly irritating title. The 'fourth mansions' to which the author refers are the dwelling-places erected by those human cultures (a tiny minority) that have succeeded in breaking out of a threefold cycle of growth and decay: 'There is what seems like a regular pattern of excavated cities. From the bottom, three cities, each more advanced in artifact and building, one atop another; then a city of total destruction: following above will be three more cities showing advance and then a fourth showing total destruction.' Later the author quotes from Saint Teresa of Avilà: 'For I have written at great length of these Mansions (the fourth), as these are they where the greatest number of souls enter. As the natural is first united with the supernatural in these, it is here that the devil can do most harm.' The quotation is apt, for beneath the zany surface of Lafferty's writing lies a vein of Roman Catholic allegory, a persistent concern for spiritual values and a disdain for human vanity (and scientific materialism).

The place is contemporary America, and the hero is a young journalist named Freddy Foley. He researches the past of a politician called Carmody Overlark, and begins to suspect that Overlark is the reincarnation of an Arab who lived five centuries before. His investigations bring him into contact with hosts of eccentric characters (all introduced with a rapidity which bewilders the reader). There are the seven irresponsible club-members known as the 'Harvesters', who carry out mind-experiments and believe themselves to be superior individuals destined to spur humankind on to its next evolutionary stage. There is a wise fat slob named Bertigrew Bagley, who is introduced thus: 'Bagley was a crackpot, but it was not an ordinary pot that had cracked. It was a giant grotesque Gothic garboon.' This man keeps a nearly-invisible dog-ape 'plappergeist' for a pet (it is a creature which can be seen from the corner of the eye). Bagley tells Freddy Foley that there are four secret brotherhoods of exceptional human beings who surround 'that malodorous worm whom we call the common man' – namely, the Pythons, the Toads, the Badgers and the Unfledged Falcons. The brain-weaving Harvesters are in fact Pythons, the would-be prophetic intelligentsia, the 'proverbial fools who rush in'. Carmody Overlark and other mysterious returnees are Toads: 'They sleep or they die under stones for years or centuries, and then they come out from under the stones.' Bagley himself is a Badger, one who entrenches in the earth and retains an ancient wisdom. And the Unfledged Falcons are the political enthusiasts, the fascist leaders-of-men who endanger all lives. Foley, one of nature's malodorous worms, is destined to be buffeted around by these superhuman characters, as the world girds itself for the ascent to a new level in history,

from the Fourth Mansions to the Fifth – or perhaps back to
the First.

First edition: New York, Ace, 1969 (paperback)
First British edition: London, Dobson, 1972 (hardcover)
Most recent edition: London, Star (paperback)

46

JOY CHANT

Red Moon and Black Mountain: The End of the House of Kendreth

A romantic fantasy epic, full of myth and passion and derring-do, this was the first published work of the British writer Joy Chant. The tale was intended for young readers – the leading characters are three middle-class English children, Oliver, Penelope and Nicholas, who find themselves magically transported to an alien land – but, as with the books of Alan Garner and Ursula Le Guin, *Red Moon and Black Mountain* has been widely enjoyed by adults. Oliver, the oldest of the children, learns to accept mature responsibilities and virtually becomes an adult hero in the course of the story (he even grows a moustache). There are lush descriptions of topography, and the imaginary societies depicted in the novel are complex and convincing. Throughout, Chant strives for an evocative and 'singing' prose style – and succeeds better than most in achieving it:

Then she stepped to the very lip of the rock, so that her skirts were blowing out over the void; and she spread her arms and held out her hands to the White Eagles, and called out to them in a language Nicholas did not understand. It was a language of cold, pure sounds; a language of words harsh and sad. It brought visions of bare shining rockscapes, of high lonely peaks, of wintry solitudes through nights of splintering cold and days of piercing light. Every word seemed to come across vast gulfs, gulfs wider than space and deeper than time; one soul speaking to another across a schism made in the very beginning of the world. Nicholas' whole body shuddered as he listened.

Her voice wavered and sank. The whole speech – it was more than a speech really, yet not quite a song – had sounded very like a lament, although it was not. But there was the same keening note in the reply of the Eagle King, fierce and chill . . .

The three youngsters are enjoying a cycle ride in the countryside one fine spring day, when a mysterious piper suddenly shifts them to the Starlit Land of Kedrinh by means of his magical tune. Oliver is separated from the others, and is shortly accepted into a tribe of plains horse-men ('Khentors'). Penelope and Nicholas find themselves on a dark and freezing mountainside, where they in turn are soon befriended and offered protection by the Princess In'serinna (she who communes with the white eagles). Many months go by before the three are reunited – with Oliver, in particular, becoming totally acclimatized to his barbarous new life. The children have arrived in the midst of a vast, earth-shaking struggle between the forces of light and darkness. The Lord of the Black Mountain has fallen from the good, and has now returned from exile to challenge the legitimate forces of the Starlit Land. His nefarious power grows with the rising of this world's Red Moon; and the three young people must each learn to play a part in the coming battle . . .

The elements from which Joy Chant has constructed her exciting story are traditional (and now thoroughly com-monplace in heroic fantasy), but here they are deployed with a rare skill and emotional conviction. As the novelist Robert Nye remarked when reviewing this book on its first publication, it has a 'confident grandeur only found in works whose authors are totally immersed in the intricacies of their own creation'.

First edition: London, Allen & Unwin, 1970 (hardcover)
First American edition: New York, Doubleday, 1970 (hardcover)
Most recent editions: New York, Ballantine, and London, Unwin (paperbacks)

47

JACK FINNEY

Time and Again

Stories of time travel, particularly those which deal with journeys into the unguessable future, are normally regarded as science fiction. But there is a sub-category, often labelled the Timeslip Romance, which has much more of the flavour of fantasy. It is an old form: Mark Twain's *A Connecticut Yankee at the Court of King Arthur* (1889) is a variant (made doubly fantastic by the fact that the world Twain's hero visits is not 'historical' but a fantasy realm conceived in the Middle Ages); several of Rider Haggard's novels are pure examples of the type – *The Ancient Allan* (1920) and *Allan and the Ice Gods* (1927) both describe trips to the ancient past by means of drugged reverie; and it is a story form which remains popular in the American cinema. Jack Finney's *Time and Again* is one of the finest modern examples of the timeslip novel. (For later variants see the entries below for Lisa Goldstein's *The Dream Years* [93] and Ken Grimwood's *Replay* [97].)

In most timeslip romances there is little attempt to rationalize the act of time travel – as often as not, it occurs as the result of the yearning of a lovelorn heart. By contrast, Finney prepares the ground very carefully indeed. His man of the present visits New York in the year 1882 as a participant in an expensive government project (an ironic inversion of the Apollo space programme, which reached its fruition at the very moment Finney was writing his book). There are a few references to Einstein, by way of a nod to the conventions of sf, but the time travel in this novel remains an arbitrarily, if elaborately, willed piece of magic. The hero, 28-year-old graphic designer Simon Morley, is invited to join a secret project which hopes to prove that all past times continue to coexist with the present day. The theory is that the present is a shared illusion, reinforced by millions of unconscious mental habits, and that one can *think* oneself into a past era simply by adopting the correct frame of mind. No time machine or similar technological gadgetry is required here, just a great deal of meticulous planning of the ground. The project's director explains to Si Morley how they have prepared a small town for another of their volunteers:

'They're ripping out all the neon, they'll tear out every dial phone, unscrew every frosted light bulb. We've carted out most of the electrical appliances already: power lawn mowers and the like. We're removing every scrap of plastic, restoring the buildings, and tearing down the few new ones. We're even *removing* the paving from certain streets, turning them back into lovely dirt roads. When we're finished, the bakery will be ready with string and white paper to wrap fresh-baked bread in. There'll be little water sprays in Gelardi's store to keep the fresh vegetables cool. The fire engine will be horse-drawn, all automobiles the right kind, and the newspaper will begin turning out daily duplicates of those it published in 1926 . . .'

A kindred effort is made to prepare an apartment in the fine old Dakota Building, New York, for Morley's trip to 1882 – and it succeeds. A moving story of love, nostalgia and mystery ensues, as the hero returns to the past again and again, finally determining to stay there forever. Jack Finney (born 1911) had a considerable success with this novel, which sold millions of copies in the United States. One can understand why: the book is impeccably constructed (and well illustrated with old magazine drawings and photographs); every detail is telling, and the plot is ingenious. It also has great atmosphere and charm.

First edition: New York, Simon & Schuster, 1970
(hardcover)
First British edition: London, Weidenfeld & Nicolson, 1980
(hardcover)
Most recent edition: New York, Simon & Schuster
(paperback)

48

JOHN GARDNER

Grendel

This unusual and ironic book proves to be the well-known story of the Anglo-Saxon epic *Beowulf*, retold from the point of view of the ugly, shambling monster Grendel. Although it ends with its protagonist's inevitable death, it is narrated in the first person, in Grendel's own bitter voice. He nurses a hatred of humankind, but is also fascinated by these vain and violent little creatures: 'As the bands grew larger they would seize and clear a hill and, with the trees they'd cut, would set up shacks, and on the crown of the hill a large, shaggy house with a steeply pitched roof and a wide stone hearth, where they'd all go at night for protection from other bands of men. The inside walls would be beautifully painted and hung with tapestries, and every cross-timber or falcon's perch was carved and gewgawed with toads, snakes, dragon shapes, deer, cows, pigs, trees, trolls . . . Then the wars began, and the war songs, and the weapon making.' Men are warlike, and detestable in their cruelty, but nevertheless Grendel is awed by their capacity for art, the ability of their poets and singers to conceive ideals which may reshape the world.

Grendel is fundamentally an honest monster – he will eat human beings when he gets the chance – and he is puzzled by men's ability to sanctify their own gory deeds. In order to discuss the human problem with another nonhuman mind, he visits an ancient dragon in his cave: 'Vast, red-golden, huge tail coiled, limbs sprawled over his treasure hoard, eyes not fiery but cold as the memory of family deaths. Vanishing away across invisible floors, there were things of gold, gems, jewels, silver vessels the colour of blood in the undulant, dragon-red light. Arching above him the ceiling and upper walls of his cave were alive with bats. The colour of his sharp scales darkened and brightened as the dragon inhaled and exhaled slowly, drawing new air across his vast internal furnace . . .' In his wisdom, the dragon can foresee a time when humankind will destroy the earth: 'A sea of black oil and dead things. No wind. No light. Nothing stirring, not even an ant, a spider. A silent universe. Such is the end of the flicker of time, the brief, hot fuse of events and ideas set off, accidentally, and snuffed out, accidentally, by man.'

But that is in the future. Meanwhile, the oft-told, tragic story unfolds. Grendel harries the human beings, but one day a valiant new warrior arrives at King Hrothgar's hall: 'He had a strange face that, little by little, grew unsettling to me . . . The eyes slanted downward, never blinking, unfeeling as a snake's. He had no more beard than a fish. He smiled as he spoke, but it was as if the gentle voice, the childlike yet faintly ironic smile were holding something back, some magician-power that could blast stone cliffs to ashes as lightning blasts trees.' Sure enough, Beowulf seems to have supernatural strength and luck: when Grendel enters the hall that night the warrior seizes his arm and tears it off at the shoulder. The wounded monster stumbles into the snowbound woods, to die surrounded by the wild animals: ' "Poor Grendel's had an accident," I whisper. "*So may you all.*"'

John Gardner (1933–82), an American teacher of Old and Middle English, wrote a number of well-received novels before his death in a motorcycle accident. Several of these verge on fantasy, particularly his last, *Mickelsson's Ghosts* (1982) – a lengthy book about an academic philosopher who sees apparitions. But the moving and poetic *Grendel* has long been his most popular novel.

First edition: New York, Knopf, 1971 (hardcover)
First British edition: London, Deutsch, 1972 (hardcover)
Most recent editions: London, Picador, and New York, Penguin (paperbacks)

49

DORIS LESSING

Briefing for a Descent into Hell

A number of Doris Lessing's novels lie on the borders of science fiction and fantasy. This particular example, which describes the voyage of a modern soul through fantastic landscapes and cosmic visions, has been accepted by many critics as one of her finest works. Lessing herself categorizes it as 'inner-space fiction – for there is never anywhere to go but in'.

The police find an unknown man wandering in London at night, apparently drugged or insane. 'Rambling, Confused and Amenable,' he is admitted to hospital, where over the coming weeks he will be treated by two well-meaning psychiatrists, Doctor X and Doctor Y. They pump him full of drugs, and attempt to establish his identity. The patient seems to be an educated man, possibly with a nautical background. He babbles of the sea and ships, but refuses to give any rational answers to his interrogators. The puzzled doctors disagree on which type of treatment will be most beneficial – one of them advocates electro-shock therapy – but they are unanimous in regarding this patient as 'mad', a deviant subject who must at all costs be returned to the normal, consensual world.

Meanwhile, the reader is privileged to enter the far more vivid world of the nameless man's fantasies. He is a heroic and solitary voyager whose small vessel tosses on the merciless waves of a vast, inner Atlantic. Like some latter-day Ancient Mariner, he is bereft of all shipmates and apparently damned to travel whither the currents will take him. After a hellish period of drifting round and around in circles, he is helped to shore by a friendly porpoise. He arrives in a magical, uninhabited South America – where two large and placid cats guide him up a dangerous cliff-path to the edge of a huge plateau. At first there are no signs of humanity, then the narrator stumbles across some worn stones which seem to be the remnants of a razed building. There follows an astonishing scene in which a ghostly city seems to spring from the ground – a city without inhabitants and without roofs, its cold rooms all open to the moonlight: 'I looked out, and was not surprised at all to see that I was surrounded by the ruins of a stone city, that stretched as far as I could see from the top of these deep stone steps. Trees grew among the buildings, and there had been gardens, for there were all kinds of flowering and scented plants everywhere, water channels ran from house to house, their cool stone beds still quite whole, and as if invisible workmen maintained them . . . And when the moon rose for the third time since I had arrived on this coast, I was wandering among the streets and avenues of stone as if I were among friends.' Here the wanderer feels compelled to clear a landing site for a crystalline spacecraft which he knows will descend in order to carry him away into the cosmos. And there he will experience a glorious and terrifying vision of life's meaning.

As all this is happening, the good Doctors X and Y continue their blind course of medication, squabbling with each other via little memoranda which punctuate the text. They discover that their patient is one Charles Watkins, a university lecturer. The name is significant, for it is possible that Doris Lessing (born 1919) has based her story on a real-life case – that of a man named Jesse Watkins, whose 'Ten-Day Voyage' through madness to a kind of wisdom was recounted in R. D. Laing's book *The Politics of Experience* (1967). Like the renegade psychiatrist Laing (who became a fashionable guru-figure in the late 1960s), Lessing believes in the spiritual value of a madness which heals, and through her artistry in this novel she convinces us (at least temporarily) of the truth in her thesis.

First edition: London, Cape, 1971 (hardcover)
First American edition: New York, Knopf, 1971 (hardcover)
Most recent editions: London, Grafton, and New York,
Random House (paperbacks)

50

ROGER ZELAZNY

Jack of Shadows

Zelazny's tale is set on a world which has ceased to rotate and hence is divided into regions of permanent night and day with a band of twilight in between. This is a common enough science-fiction situation, used for example by Brian Aldiss in *Hothouse* (1962), by Michael Moorcock in *The Twilight Man* (1966) and by J.G. Ballard in his haunting short story 'The Day of Forever' (1966). But all of those were set on our Earth: Roger Zelazny does not indicate whether the action of his novel is placed in the far future or the distant past, or indeed on a world in some alternative universe. Nor does it matter, for this is not a work with a science fiction rationale but one which follows the logic of fantasy and has the timeless quality of pure romance.

Much of the action takes place on the dark side of the world, where magic rules. The hero, Jack, is a picaresque rogue who uses his supernatural powers in a quest for vengeance which turns into something larger than he expected. In the course of the narrative he travels through the 'night' and the 'day' realms, growing in awareness and ambition as he does so, and eventually he harnesses both the science of day and the magic of night to further his ends. *Jack of Shadows* follows the traditional pattern of picaresque tales – in which an exiled hero goes in search of his real name, the truth of his parentage, the solution to the conundrum of his own existence. As in Poul Anderson's *Three Hearts and Three Lions*, wherein a man of mysterious birth is snatched from one world in order to become the saviour of another, Zelazny's Jack comes to know himself and the nature of his quest. He even has an externalized 'soul' which follows him around throughout the last quarter of the book; and he also has a father figure in the form of the great stone god Morningstar, who on the last page is shown with outstretched hands waiting to catch Jack as he falls from the battlements of his castle.

Like most of Zelazny's work, *Jack of Shadows* is written in a laconic and faintly tongue-in-cheek style, full of witticisms and poeticisms. This is a writer of considerable linguisitic resource, although one feels that his talents are not being stretched to the full in this beguiling but rather lightweight novel. Occasionally the action moves too fast; Zelazny skimps and gives us perfunctory scenes. Nevertheless there are many engaging and ingenious moments – such as the incident of Jack's imprisonment in a jewel which hangs around the neck of his arch enemy, the Lord of Bats.

This is a free-standing novel, and effective as such. The best-known contribution to modern fantasy by Roger Zelazny (born 1937) is his so-called 'Amber' series – *Nine Princes in Amber* (1970), *The Guns of Avalon* (1972), *Sign of the Unicorn* (1975), *The Hand of Oberon* (1976), *The Courts of Chaos* (1978), and so on in an apparently endless sequence. These novels, about the internecine squabbles of a group of princelings in the hidden, parallel world known as Amber, are highly readable and entertaining at first, but they begin to pall as one realizes the nature of the card-shuffling game which the author is playing.

First edition: New York, Walker, 1971 (hardcover)
First British edition: London, Faber, 1972 (hardcover)
Most recent edition: New York, NAL (paperback)

51

RICHARD ADAMS

Watership Down

After *The Lord of the Rings*, this is probably the most successful fantasy novel of recent times – certainly the most successful by a British writer. Like Tolkein's book, it was a 'sleeper', an unknown author's eccentric work which went on to confound all its publishers' expectations. It sold in huge quantities, and despite the book's implicit conservatism it seems to have appealed to younger adults, the ecologically-aware hippy generation of the late sixties and early seventies (much the same group of people who had turned Tolkien into a belated best-seller just a few years earlier). Richard Adams (born 1920) was a civil servant by profession and has always been a countryman at heart. His book is about talking rabbits, and it fits squarely in the tradition of such 'animal classics' as Kenneth Grahame's *The Wind in the Willows* (1908).

It is a long novel, full of loving detail and narrated in epic style. The central characters are a courageous young rabbit named Hazel, and his second-sighted brother Fiver. They live in a crowded warren which is run in dictatorial fashion by the Chief Rabbit and his *Owsla* – a 'group of strong or clever rabbits – second-year or older – surrounding the Chief Rabbit and his doe and exercising authority' (the book is full of such invented terms). Nervous little Fiver has a scary premonition that doom is about to be visited upon the warren, and at first only his brother Hazel is inclined to believe him. They attempt to persuade the Chief Rabbit of the need for action, but he brushes them off. A notice-board has been erected at the foot of the hill which houses

146

the warren, and the reader is told its message – 'This ideally situated estate is to be developed with highclass modern residences' – which confirms Fiver's far-sightedness.

Hazel decides to lead Fiver and a group of discontented young rabbits away from the warren. These companions have names such as Bigwig, Dandelion and Pipkin. With difficulty, they evade the patrolling *Owsla* and make their escape by night. They have embarked on a vast journey (in reality, a distance of just a few miles across the Berkshire countryside) which is fraught with terrifying dangers. 'The very plants were unknown to them – pink lousewort with its sprays of hooked flowers, bog asphodel and the thin-stemmed blooms of the sun-dews, rising above their hairy, fly-catching mouths, all shut fast by night. In this close jungle all was silence.' Along the way, they hearten them-selves with tales of El-ahrairah, the mythical rabbit hero. They encounter human beings, predatory animals, fast-flowing streams and many other perils, including other colonies of rabbits. But eventually, thanks to Hazel's wise leadership, they reach the pastoral haven of Watership Down, where – in time, after they have won a great battle against the minions of General Woundwort (a sort of rabbit Hitler) – they will found a new warren.

It is easy to mock *Watership Down* for being an over-inflated children's novel. It was Adams's book which inspired Michael Moorcock's delightful quip: 'if the bulk of American sf could be said to be written by robots, about robots, for robots, then the bulk of English fantasy seems to be written by rabbits, about rabbits and for rabbits' (repeated in his *Wizardry and Wild Romance,* 1987). Never-theless it is a novel which has pleased millions of readers, and it is not difficult to see why. It is a very accomplished quest narrative (and war story), combined with a moving tract on behalf of nature conservation.

First edition: London, Rex Collings, 1972 (hardcover)
First American edition: New York, Macmillan, 1974 (hardcover)
Most recent editions: London, Penguin, and New York, Avon (paperbacks)

52

ANGELA CARTER

The Infernal Desire Machines of Doctor Hoffman

Angela Carter (born 1940) is England's foremost Gothicist, author of a book on the Marquis de Sade as well as a number of darkly fantastic novels and story-collections – *The Magic Toyshop* (1967), *Love* (1971), *Fireworks* (1974) and *The Bloody Chamber* (1979), among others. Her unmistakable prose style – heavily adjectival, languorous and erotic, dreamlike yet curiously precise – shows the influence of nineteenth-century French literature: not only Sade, but Baudelaire, Rimbaud, Huysmans, the *Symbolistes* and the early members of the surrealist movement. She has also been influenced by the cinema, from German expressionism to Hollywood sentimentality. Yet she remains stubbornly British and individualistic, a pragmatic metaphysician with a puckish sense of humour. *The Infernal Desire Machines of Doctor Hoffman* is the best of Carter's early novels, the one which stretches her unique blend of talents to the full.

It is the first-person narrative of a young man named Desiderio, who works as a government servant in some imaginary Latin American republic. His city is suffering a plague of illusions, which have apparently been unleashed by the mysterious renegade scientist, Dr Hoffman. The opening pages of Desiderio's account are reminiscent of a William Burroughs nightmare of bureaucracy run wild: 'I was the confidential secretary to the Minister of Determination, who wanted to freeze the entire freak show the city had become back into attitudes of perfect propriety. The Minister sent the Determination Police round to break all the mirrors because of the lawless images they were disseminating.' But despite the Minister's ruthlessness the authorities are losing their war against the emanations of 'eroto-energy' which are being pumped into the urban air by Dr Hoffman's hidden machines. Things are rapidly falling apart, and Hoffman's 'ambassador' (who is really his beautiful daughter, Albertina, in disguise) warns the Minister: 'Prepare yourself for a long, immense and deliberate derangement of the senses.' But it is Desiderio who is to bear the brunt of this derangement, when he sets out on a one-man mission to locate the mad scientist and perhaps kill him.

The description of Desiderio's lengthy journey is an imaginative *tour de force*, its stations marked by the oneiric chapter titles Carter has chosen: 'The Mansions of Midnight', 'The Acrobats of Desire', 'The Erotic Traveller', 'The Coast of Africa', 'Lost in Nebulous Time'. Throughout his quest, our hero is haunted by visions of Albertina, who appears to him in various guises, whipping him into a fever of sexual longing. En route he encounters a hallucinatory peepshow, an extremely libidinous circus troupe, a Count Dracula figure who defies the universe with his monstrous and insatiable appetites, a tribe of African cannibals, and a community of tattooed centaurs. The vivid details of the centaurs' life are on a par with Swift's evocation of the Houyhnhnms in *Gulliver*: 'These hippolators believed their god revealed himself to them in the droppings excreted by the horse part of themselves since this manifested the purest essence of their equine natures. The twice daily movement of their bowels was at once a form of prayer and a divine communion.' Eventually the lovely Albertina reveals herself to Desiderio and leads him to her father's castle, where it turns out that Dr Hoffman has been encouraging the young man's lust in order to provide yet more fuel for his infernal desire machines. All this may remind us of Freud as interpreted by Universal Film Studios, but in fact it is a vision which could have come from no other mind but Angela Carter's.

First edition: London, Hart-Davis, 1972 (hardcover)
First American edition: New York, Harcourt Brace Jovanovich, 1974 (hardcover; as *The War of Dreams*)
Most recent edition; Harmondsworth, Penguin (paperback)

53

MICHAEL FRAYN

Sweet Dreams

Here we have yet another novel about the life which follows death – the modern fantasist's favourite theme? – though this one is very different in tone from all those that have been written before and since. Thirty-seven-year-old Englishman Howard Baker, accurately described by his friend as 'the collective imagination of the middle classes compressed into one pair of trousers', dies in a car smash and goes straight to Heaven (naturally). It turns out to be a very English and very middle-class Heaven: a rather more beatific version of 1970s London, full of fine roadways, grand architecture and all modern conveniences. Our joyful hero discovers that he can fly: 'Howard is enchanted by the slowness with which he can move, and the smallness of the gestures which are needed to change course and height. He steers himself into the current of warm air rising above the chandelier, and is carried effortlessly upwards, past the floors where people are sitting at little tables and eating icecream out of metal goblets. Some of them smile at him, and wave. "This is fantastic!" he shouts.' But he soon gives this up as a childish prank, and settles down to the serious middle-class business of finding a job, establishing a home, raising a family, and planning his career in the afterlife.

Everything comes easily, as it should in Heaven. He goes to work for a design agency whose current commission from God is to design the Alps. In a fit of inspiration, Howard comes up with the design concept for the Matterhorn, an achievement which makes his name in the profession. ('It's a real young man's mountain, of course. He

never does anything quite so bold again, or quite so fast.')
Despite his material success, a sweetly compliant family
and an endless round of good-natured dinner-parties (with
apple crumble for afters), Howard begins to feel stirrings
of discontent. Why should his lot in the afterlife be so
happy – especially since the living world is still mired in
misery? He is developing a fine social conscience, and he
proceeds to write a report on the human condition which
will amount to a damning exposé of God's unjust system.
Unfortunately, this being Heaven, all Howard's efforts
persist in turning out for the best: 'The first two impres-
sions of the report sell out before publication, and there is
fierce competition for the paperback rights. The reviews
are marvellous, and Howard gets a call from Bill Mishkin,
of Bill Mishkin Productions.' Disgusted by his own success, Howard decides to live simply in the country. He
becomes a rural sage, writes letters to the press on the great
issues of the day, and appears on television. But all too
soon the social whirl of Heaven catches up with him again.
At last he is privileged to meet God (in a hilarious scene),
and it turns out that God has a special appointment in mind
for him: 'What I thought was that we could fix you up with
some sort of nominal job in the organization.' Howard's
days as a rebel are over: he has finally arrived at the pinnacle
of Heavenly bliss.

Michael Frayn (born 1933) is a well-known English
novelist, playwright, humorist and broadcaster. *Sweet
Dreams* is probably his best book – a beautifully sustained
satire on the limitations of middle-class good intentions,
reasonableness, decency, selflessness, moderation, fairness,
sound common sense and all-round good-chappery. It is
impeccably written, profound (and perhaps depressing) in
its implications, and very, very funny.

First edition: London, Collins, 1973 (hardcover)
*First American edition:*New York, Viking, 1974 (hardcover)
Most recent edition: London, Fontana (paperback)

54

PATRICIA A. McKILLIP

The Forgotten Beasts of Eld

McKillip is an American writer whose first novel is a fairy-tale work, written in dreamy style. It is the story of the lonely 'ice-maiden' Sybel, who lives high in the hills, far from the workaday world. She is the great-granddaughter of a wizard, and inheritor of a collection of fabulous, heraldic beasts. In bygone years, her father and grandfather have put together a menagerie of enchanted creatures: the Black Swan of Tirlith, a 'great-winged, golden-eyed bird'; the Boar Cyrin, 'who knew the answers to all riddles save one'; Gyld, the winged dragon; the Lyon Gules; the Cat Moriah; the Falcon Ter; and so on. Sybel's father has taught her how to communicate with these fearsome but loyal beasts, and how to control them by means of telepathy. 'He died when she was sixteen, leaving her alone with the beautiful white house, a vast library of heavy, iron-bound books, a collection of animals beyond dreaming, and the power to hold them.' Sybel remains virginal, and has no time for human beings.

Men try to force their way into her private world. When she is sixteen, a handsome red-haired soldier arrives one night at her gate. He carries a baby, and pleads with her to give it protection. Reluctantly, she takes the boy-child in, and the soldier leaves. The baby is named Tamlorn – 'My Tam,' as Sybel comes to call him – and over the next twelve years he grows to be a sturdy lad. The soldier returns, bearing a message: Tamlorn is a prince who must claim his birthright. Sybel has grown to love the boy, and she resists the world's demands fiercely – even though she feels strangely attracted to the bearer of the message, who soon declares his own love for her. She spurns the man, hating the warlike culture which he represents, but she remains troubled by the matter of her foster-son's destiny. Later, she calls the king, Tamlorn's father, to her (Sybel has the magical ability to 'summon' human beings as well as beasts) – and allows him to take the boy away. The king, too, falls in love with her, and offers to make her a queen; however, she is determined to retain her independence, alone in her high icy castle. The frustrated king sets a magician against her, but she is able to overcome this danger. Eventually she gives her heart to the king's rival, the soldier who first brought her the baby. Various political consequences follow, but the main thrust of the story concerns Sybel's emotional development, her discovery of herself. When she and her new husband fly on the back of the Dragon Gyld, it is a kind of fulfilment:

> The great wings unfurled, black against the stars. The huge bulk lifted slowly, incredibly, away from the cold earth, through the wind-torn, whispering trees. Above the winds struck full force, billowing their cloaks, pushing against them, and they felt the immense play of muscle beneath them and the strain of wing against wind. Then came the full, smooth, joyous soar, a drowning in wind and space, a spiralling descent into darkness.

The Forgotten Beasts of Eld is a beautifully sustained fantasy – wise, sweet-toned and gentle, without being too cloying. It is a 'girl's book', a menarche fantasy, although it has a broader appeal than that label might suggest. Patricia McKillip may have been influenced to some extent by the juvenile romances of Andre Norton and Anne McCaffrey, but she is a better writer then most who have produced work in this vein. Her later books include the trilogy which consists of *Riddlemaster of Hed* (1976), *Heir of*

Sea and Fire (1977) and *Harpist in the Wind* (1979) – romantic high fantasies of a delicate kind.

First edition: New York, Ballantine, 1974 (paperback)
First British edition: London, Futura, 1987 (paperback)

55

STEPHEN KING

'Salem's Lot

Stephen King made his name with *Carrie* (1974), the tale of a persecuted young girl who is gifted with terrifying destructive powers. In the wake of *Rosemary's Baby* and *The Exorcist*, King's first novel did very well, both as a book and as a film. He swiftly followed it up with *'Salem's Lot*, a much bulkier tome which is his homage to the Dracula legend. The setting is a little New England town called Jerusalem's Lot (''salem's' for short), in the present day. Here a big old derelict house, 'the Marsten place', is taken over by a mysterious newcomer who proves to be a vampire from the classic mould. This reclusive Mr Barlow gradually infects the entire village with the disease of vampirism, turning its 1300 inhabitants into a colony of the undead. The viewpoint shifts, but the story is told mainly through the eyes of Ben Mears, a 32-year-old writer who has just returned to the town after spending his adult lifetime elsewhere.

What turns this clichéd scenario into a highly effective tale of terror is the careful development of the characters. And this applies not only to Ben Mears and the girl with whom he strikes up a relationship; for here it is an entire community that comes into contact with the supernatural, not just some unfortunate individual or tiny group. King excels in the depiction of 'plain folks' – housewives, teenagers, the local milkman, the cemetery ground-keeper, the real-estate agent, the schoolteacher, the drunken priest and, above all, the kids:

The door shut softly and his father's slippered feet descended the stairs.

He found himself reflecting – not for the first time – on the peculiarity of adults. They took laxatives, liquor, or sleeping pills to drive away their terrors so that sleep would come, and their terrors were so tame and domestic: the job, the money, does my wife still love me, who are my friends. They were pallid compared to the fears every child lies cheek and jowl with in his dark bed, with no one to confess to in hope of perfect understanding but another child. There is no group therapy or psychiatry or community social services for the child who must cope with the thing under the bed or in the cellar every night, the thing which leers and capers and threatens just beyond the point where vision will reach. The same lonely battle must be fought night after night and the only cure is the eventual ossification of the imaginary faculties, and this is called adulthood.

'Salem's Lot has been filmed, as has virtually all of the author's work (in this case it formed the basis of a lengthy television movie directed by Tobe Hooper in 1979). Stephen King (born 1947) is reputed to be the most commercially successful novelist in the history of American publishing, and most of this popularity has been built on his exploitation of fantasy motifs. He is not a very original writer, but he is an immensely skilful one. His novels are frequently slapdash but they do tend to contain something for everyone: not only the traditional horror ingredients, but sharp characterization, large elements of everyday realism, warm family sentiment, mystery, a sympathy for children, physical disgust (what King likes to call the 'grossout'), excellent story-telling rhythm, humour, and an engaging, chatty tone of voice. His work seems to have an equally powerful appeal for male and female readers – and that, above all, is the reason for its colossal market success.

First edition: New York, Doubleday, 1975 (hardcover)
First British edition: London, NEL, 1976 (hardcover)
Most recent editions: New York, NAL and London, NEL (paperbacks)

56

BRIAN MOORE

The Great Victorian Collection

Brian Moore (born 1921) is an Irish-Canadian novelist of distinction, author of *The Luck of Ginger Coffey* (1960) and *The Doctor's Wife* (1976) among other highly-praised realistic works. He has written several books in a fantastic vein – for example, *Fergus* (1971), about a writer who is haunted by ghosts from his guilty past, and the supernatural thriller *Cold Heaven*. *The Great Victorian Collection* is one of Moore's finest novels, an amusing and engrossing fable about the fate of the marvellous in our matter-of-fact society.

Anthony Maloney, an assistant professor of history and an expert in all things Victorian, checks into the Sea Winds Motel in Carmel, California. He has been attending a seminar at Berkeley, and intends to leave for Canada within a couple of days. However, his sojourn at the motel is destined to last many months, as a result of the remarkable event which takes place during his first night there. As he sleeps, he dreams that he awakes and looks through his window on to the motel's previously empty parking lot:

The lot resembled a crowded open-air market, a maze of narrow lanes lined with stalls, some permanently roofed, some draped in green tarpaulin awnings. I unfastened the catch of the window and eased myself onto a wooden outdoor staircase. I began to walk along what seemed to be the central aisle of the market, an aisle dominated by a glittering crystal fountain, its columns of polished glass soaring to the height of a telegraph pole. Laid out on the

159

stalls and in partially enclosed exhibits resembling furniture showrooms was the most astonishing collection of Victorian artefacts, *objets d'art*, furniture, household appliances, paintings, jewellery, scientific instruments, toys, tapestries, sculpture, handicrafts, woollen and linen samples, industrial machinery, ceramics, silverware, books, furs, men's and women's clothing, musical instruments, a huge telescope mounted on a pedestal, a railway locomotive, marine equipment, small arms, looms, bric-a-brac, and curiosa.

Then he *really* wakes up – only to look out of the window and find that his dream has come true. The incredible collection of Victoriana is there, somehow conjured into existence by his sleeping mind.

Maloney cannot believe his luck. Feverishly, he inspects the valuable objects – which are full of an inexpressible pathos when so far removed from their original time and place – but soon discovers that if he attempts to take any of them from the parking lot they immediately deteriorate and become 'fakes'. The collection must remain *in situ:* it must be covered, guarded, preserved, and eventually exploited. The remainder of the novel deals with the consequences of this miracle. We never learn why the exhibition materialized in the first place – it is simply a given, like Gregor Samsa's transformation into a beetle at the beginning of Kafka's 'The Metamorphosis'. Instead, the story describes, in logical, realistic, and frequently comical fashion, the reactions of all those who come in contact with Maloney and his glorious heap of Victoriana. It tells how the collection becomes a media sensation, a scientific conundrum, a seven days' wonder, a sideshow, and at length an all-but-forgotten curiosity. It also tells how the great Victorian collection destroys its 'creator'. Interpret it how you will (and of course it is tempting to view it as an allegory of the novelist's fate in the modern world), Moore's book is an elegant, ironic and touching parable.

First edition: New York, Farrar, Straus & Giroux, 1975 (hardcover)
First British edition: London, Cape, 1975 (hardcover)
Most recent editions: Harmondsworth, Penguin, and New York, Dutton (paperbacks)

57

Grimus

The unknown Salman Rushdie (born 1947, in India) submitted this novel to a Gollancz science fiction competition in 1974. It did not win, because it was adjudged to be pure fantasy rather than sf; but the publishers sensed that they had made a notable discovery and they gladly issued the book a year later. It was largely ignored at the time, although Ursula Le Guin did describe it as 'beautiful, funny and endlessly surprising'. Six years later Rushdie won Britain's leading literary award, the Booker Prize for Fiction, for his second novel, *Midnight's Children* (1981) – and was hailed as a major writer. *Grimus* bears small resemblance to the author's later works, but it remains an interesting piece of fantasy in its own right: amusing, philosophical, cranky, lyrical, occasionally sophomoric and always highly imaginative. It is slightly reminiscent of Angela Carter's *The Infernal Desire Machines of Dr Hoffman* (*52*), with an added dash of Kurt Vonnegut's cute jokiness.

The hero is a Red Indian who takes the name of Flapping Eagle. He enjoys an innocent existence, secure in his incestuous love for his older sister Bird-Dog, until the day the latter meets a travelling magician called Mr Sispy. This man bestows eternal life on the sister and the brother, but he also steals Bird-Dog away at dead of night. The ignorant and ill-equipped Flapping Eagle is obliged to go out into the wide world in search of Mr Sispy and the errant Bird-Dog. He becomes a gigolo, and many years go by before his elderly mistress dies and bequeathes him her money.

Flapping Eagle, as young and handsome as ever, sets sail in a borrowed yacht:

> He was the leopard who changed his spots, he was the worm that turned. He was the shifting sands and the ebbing tide. He was moody as the sky, circular as the seasons, nameless as glass. He was Chameleon, change-ling, all things to all men and nothing to any man. He had become his enemies and eaten his friends. He was all of them and none of them.
>
> He was the eagle, prince of birds; and he was also the albatross. She clung round his neck and died, and the mariner became the albatross.
>
> Having little option, he survived, wheeling his craft from shore to unsung shore, earning his keep, filling the empty hours of the hollow days of the vacant years. Contentment without contents, achievement without goal, these were the paradoxes that swallowed him.

Eventually he falls through a 'hole in the Mediterranean into that other sea, that not-quite-Mediterranean' which belongs to a different dimension of space and time – and there he arrives at Calf Island. Here, in the mountaintop city of K, dwells Grimus, a mysterious master of ceremonies; and here the drama of Flapping Eagle's search for sister, self and a sense of reality will be played out. He is helped in his long climb up the mountainside by Mr Virgil Jones, a schoolmasterly figure who has a love of puns and Latin tags. The latter also has an understanding of the various metaphysical snares and delusions which await all climbers. They meet many new characters, including inter-dimensional entities, and many revenants – before the various parts of Flapping Eagle's shattered personality come together in a suitably apocalyptic climax. Rushdie's is an ambiguous and at times irritating novel, written in the manner of a fantastic folk-tale but clearly the product of a very modern, ironic and cosmopolitan intelligence.

First edition: London, Gollancz, 1975 (hardcover)
First American edition: New York, Overlook Press, 1979 (hardcover)
Most recent edition: London, Granada (paperback)

58

GENE WOLFE

Peace

This moving and delicately written novel begins in deceptive fashion: 'The elm tree planted by Eleanor Bold, the judge's daughter, fell last night. I was asleep and heard nothing.' The speaker is Alden Dennis Weer, a man of about sixty whose story we are going to hear. It gradually dawns on us, as we read this narrative of a quiet Midwestern life, that Alden Weer is probably a ghost, dead before the book even begins. Perhaps he is unable to rest in peace until he has paid this homage to all the people and forces that have shaped his existence.

The author's deceptions continue. We expect a straightforward life story, but in fact Weer has surprisingly little to say about himself. The digressions proliferate, to such an extent that they form the bulk of the novel. Subsidiary characters take over the action, and we are treated to tales within tales – some of them Chinese or Irish in flavour, but most of them American and all brilliantly told. The connections between the apparently disparate parts are subtle: the reader has to glean for clues all the way, and this may prove an irksome task to some. It is definitely not a book for the impatient. But the rewards are rich for those who persevere; and I have no hesitation in proclaiming Gene Wolfe's novel a masterpiece.

We meet Weer's mother and grandfather and nursemaid (all now dead). We also meet his eccentric aunt Olivia, a truly wonderful character, and her three ardent suitors. We hear the tale of each suitor's life, and enjoy his words, his tall stories, his sharply individual voice. All are now dead, and we come to realize that what we are reading is in fact a 'Book of the Dead', or, more exactly (in a deliberate nod to H.P. Lovecraft), it is a version of *The Necronomicon*, the Book That Binds the Dead. All these dead voices speak out of the past, claiming no more than the fact that they existed, they *were*; and amid all the humour and quirkiness the final effect is one of great pathos.

In an early scene young Alden Weer goes for a picnic with his Aunt Olivia and one of her suitors, Professor Peacock. They visit a cave, where each of them in turn notices a human skull and decides not to mention it. 'The Indians lived here, didn't they?' asks the boy. 'Pre-Indians,' says the Professor. 'The aboriginal people who – about ten thousand years ago – crossed the Bering Strait and eventually settled at Indianola, Indian Lake, Indianapolis, and various other places, at which points they were forced to become Indians in order to justify the place-names.' Much, much later, in nearly the last scene of the novel, Weer listens to an old farmer who laments the passing of traditional agricultural ways: 'My own farm – when I'm gone it's gone. Had three boys and none of them want it.' These anecdotes, and dozens of others throughout the novel, carry the same burden: untold thousands of lives have gone before, each with its own story and its own idiosyncratic voice.

Wolfe assumes many of those voices in this beautiful book, and his ear for oral tale-telling is superb. We come to believe in all these dead people; we feel their vibrant life. Gene Wolfe (born 1931) is now well-known for his *Book of the New Sun* tetralogy (1980–3) and for such recent fantasies as *Free Live Free* (1984) and *Soldier of the Mist* (1986). *Peace* is a comparatively neglected early work – quiet, understated, and probably unsurpassable.

First edition: New York, Harper & Row, 1975 (hardcover)
First British edition: London, Chatto & Windus, 1984 (hardcover)
Most recent editions: New York, Berkley, and London, NEL (paperbacks)

59

BRIAN ALDISS

The Malacia Tapestry

'We may enjoy the present while we are insensible of infirmity and decay; but the present, like a note in music, is nothing but as it appertains to what is past and what is to come.' So wrote Walter Savage Landor in the nineteenth century. Brian Aldiss, prose-poet of fecundity threatened by entropy, has said that he finds this quotation resonant, and indeed Landor's sombre sentiment seems to underlie much of the surface slap-and-tickle, the at times rather desperate *joie de vivre*, of Aldiss's fiction. This was never more apparent than in his major fantasy novel *The Malacia Tapestry*:

> It was Bedalar who spoke next, in a dreamy voice. 'Somebody told me that Satan has decided to close the world down, and the magicians have agreed. What would happen wouldn't be unpleasant at all, but just ordinary life going on more and more slowly until it stopped absolutely.'
> 'Like a clock stopping,' Armida suggested.
> 'More like a tapestry,' Bedalar said. 'I mean one day like today, things might run down and never move again, so that we and everything would hang there like a tapestry in the air for ever more.'

Armida and Bedalar are two beautiful, high-born girls who are courted by the young actors, 'mountebanks in an urban landscape', Perian de Chirolo and Guy de Lambant. De Chirolo is the narrator of the novel, a randy and carefree charmer who moves with perfect insouciance through a city filled with riches and glamour, poverty and plague. Malacia has existed for millennia, apparently without social change. It is vaguely Levantine and late-medieval in atmosphere (Byzantium is a neighbour, the Turks are the enemy, people refer to the goddess Minerva and other figures from Graeco-Roman mythology; but they also drink coffee). Soothsayers and priests abound; all mechanical innovations and new ideas are outlawed. More remarkably, tame dinosaurs walk the streets and are accepted as the 'ancestors' of the city's populace; winged men and women flit across the sky, from dome to spire. Malacia is one vast market-place and showground: actors, impresarios, puppeteers, artists and craftsmen all compete for the favours of the aristocracy. This is a society which is lively but static, hanging (as Bedalar suggests) like a tapestry.

In pursuit of the lovely Armida, de Chirolo becomes involved with a cranky socialist inventor who persuades the young man to act in a 'mercurized' play which will be recorded by a marvellous new machine, the 'zahnoscope'. The inventor hopes that this rudimentary form of cinema will have a revolutionary impact on Malacian life. The inevitable trouble ensues. It is a large and well-orchestrated novel, and throughout Aldiss explores the theme of the artist as middleman in the continual trade between fecundity and entropy. The story is told at a leisurely pace, and there is much humour. At the climax de Chirolo goes to Armida's family estate to hunt a 'devil-jaw' (which is to say, a *Tyrannosaurus rex*) and succeeds in attaining self-knowledge. There is no attempt to place Malacia in any logical alternative universe. The book is a deliberate fantasia of anachronism, an ahistorical potpourri. It is partly a work of heroic fantasy – after all, the protagonist slays a 'dragon', and with the aid of 'magic' – but it is also a social novel, a tale of love and snobbery, of hypergamy and class tension. The rich descriptive passages owe something to both Dickens and Mervyn Peake. Brian Aldiss (born 1925), author of many science fiction stories and comic/realistic novels, has never written anything else quite like this.

First edition: London, Cape, 1976 (hardcover)
First American edition: New York, Harper & Row, 1977 (hardcover)
Most recent edition: London, Granada (paperback)

60

GORDON R. DICKSON

The Dragon and the George

Dickson's light-hearted adventure story is dedicated to his friend Poul Anderson – 'Thys boke is for Bela of East-march, who hath in hys own time known a dragon or two' – and indeed it does owe a small debt to Anderson's *Three Hearts and Three Lions*. First published in much shorter form in *The Magazine of Fantasy and Science Fiction* in 1957, *The Dragon and the George* is the tale of Jim Eckert, a college volleyball player and expert in medieval history, who is thrown into a magical world of knightly romance. But there is a humorous twist: unlike Poul Anderson's similar hero, Eckert loses his human shape – and finds himself trapped in the form of a huge be-winged dragon.

Jim Eckert is in pursuit of his girlfriend Angie, who mysteriously 'apported' from the college's psychology lab-oratory as a result of an ill-advised experiment in astral projection. Jim, too, submits to the apportation equipment, and awakes to find himself in a cave with someone – or something – roaring at him:

'WAKE UP, GORBASH!'

An enormous head with crocodile-sized jaws equipped with larger-than-crocodile-sized fangs thrust itself between Jim's eyes and the ceiling.

'I'm awake. I – ' What he was seeing suddenly regis-tered on Jim's stunned mind and he burst out involun-tarily, 'A dragon!'

'And just what would you expect your maternal grand-uncle to be, a sea-lizard? Or are you having nightmares again? Wake up. It's Smrgol talking to you, boy. Smrgol! Come on, shake a wing and get flapping.'

Luckily, Grand-Uncle Smrgol turns out to be a kindly old soul who, in a befuddled way, gives Jim (alias Gorbash) invaluable help in his quest. It seems that one of the other dragons has captured a 'george' – that is, a human being – and of course it turns out that this unfortunate person is none other than the beautiful Angie. The wicked dragon carries her away to the Loathly Tower in the western fens. Jim, still in hulking dragon form, is obliged to give chase, while taking great delight in his new-found aerial powers.

But first he has to gain the assistance of a bad-tempered wizard, who grumbles about 'dragons galumphing hither and yon – knights galumphing yon and hither – naturals, giants, orges, sandmirks, and other sports and freaks each doing their billy-be-exorcized best to terrorize his own little part of the landscape.' Our hero advises this man to drink milk in order to calm his stomach ulcer, and in return Jim receives some magical help. Before making for the Loathly Tower, he must gather together a suitable band of Companions; and this he does, in the course of many diverting adventures. His friends and advisers include a bold (but none-too-bright) knight in armour called Neville-Smythe; a gigantic wolf; and a lovely red-haired girl who is expert with bow and arrow. Eventually they make their way to 'the ruined, dark and shattered shell of a tower as black as jet' – where they encounter, and overcome, a foe much more terrifying than any renegade dragon. They also succeed in rescuing the fair maiden, Angie.

Although Gordon R. Dickson (born 1923) first conceived this good-humoured story in the 1950s, *The Dragon and the George* may be seen as one of the novels which heralded a new wave of 'light' fantasies in the latter part of the seventies. These are best exemplified by Piers Anthony's highly popular 'Xanth' series which began with *A Spell for*

Chameleon (1977). A British equivalent is the very funny sequence of 'Discworld' novels by Terry Pratchett, commencing with *The Colour of Magic* (1983).

First edition: New York, Ballantine, 1976 (paperback)

61

EMMA TENNANT

Hotel de Dream

Dreams within dreams within dreams. At a seedy little
English hotel the guests lie in their separate rooms, dreaming their all-too-limited dreams of freedom and gratification. The ageing Mr Poynter dreams of a perfect city,
where he is awoken each morning by a 'medley of Churchill
speeches, Vera Lynn and snatches of *ITMA*'. It is a city run
with military precision, and where he is dictator of all he
surveys: 'he went through the palace, brushing aside the
A.D.C. with his usual list of requests and smiling benevo-
lently at the bowing flunkeys arranged against the walls.'
In another room, Miss Briggs dreams of Royal Garden
Parties, where the Queen of England introduces her to
celebrated actors and scientists: 'the famous names bowed
and curtsied with reverence and Miss Briggs's smile went
unchanging from one to the other.' In a third room, a
strange young schoolteacher named Jeanette Scranton
dreams of Amazon-like giantesses, nude sea-bathing and
erotic rituals. And in yet another room a lady novelist holds
conversation with her imaginary characters.

No wonder that all these people want to escape into ideal
worlds. The Westringham Hotel is a shabby-genteel
London boarding-house which is almost monstrous in its
emblematic dreadfulness. It is presided over by the imperi-
ous Mrs Routledge, who worries about 'the peculiarity of
the residents, who seemed perfectly ordinary on admission
but soon started to sleep obsessively, as if the doomed
atmosphere of the area had turned the modest hotel into

some latter-day temple to Aesculapius.' And it is maintained by a filthy old servant named Cridge:

> Mrs Routledge peered down the dark stairs that led from the dining-room of the Westringham Hotel to the black basement where her servant lived. She was used to the smell, which was like stagnant water at the bottom of an enamel pitcher and a horrible sweetness thrown in, the effect of Cridge's tobacco on the stale, damp air, but this morning it was particularly sickening. Cridge had a habit of defecating in a selection of antique jars and vases stored there and forgotten by a former resident, and on Thursdays he would come up, go through the dining-room with them and empty them in the Gentleman's Cloaks behind the reception desk in the front hall.

But even the disgusting Cridge, symbol of the lower orders in this middle-class hell, is soon recruited into the dreamers' fantasies – and the dreams begin to cross over, to merge, and to infect 'reality'. A sandy Miss Scranton, dazed by her own erotic reveries, strays from her wild beach party into Mr Poynter's trim, militaristic utopia. The lady novelist's characters rebel against the all-too-predictable life she has given them, and enlist Cridge in an attempt to assassinate her. Gradually the dreams of the hotel's occupants leak out into the world at large:

> There began to creep out of the doors and into the streets and over the countryside the faint, invisible strands of these dreams, which came down in ghostly loops over the innocent and the unsuspecting and the corrupt alike. Stockbrokers and barristers wandered half the day in Mr Poynter's City, eyes glazed and expressions abstracted as they passed under Grecian porticoes. Housewives and women at desks in offices saw suddenly long beaches, and a flat warm sea, and felt sand encrusted on their wrists and their legs heavy. Royalty breathed out from newspapers and magazines, enveloping and protecting

and carrying their prey to an unchanging and benevolent world.'

Emma Tennant (born 1938) has produced an entertaining fable which is at once a satire on the declining English scene and an allegory of the way in which we all try to recruit each other to our dreams of a better world. The result is sharp, funny and a trifle malicious.

First edition: London, Gollancz, 1976 (hardcover)
Most recent edition: London, Faber (paperback)

62

ANGELA CARTER

The Passion of New Eve

What a mind Angela Carter has! And what a talent. This intense fantasia on the possibilities of women's liberation is a wicked novel – 'wicked' in its honesty about erotic and sadistic impulses, and the ways in which those impulses subvert all our utopian dreams. Set against the haunting background of a crumbling United States of America, it is a work of pure Gothic extremism. In subject-matter, it bears a slight resemblance to Gore Vidal's *Myra Breckinridge* (1968) – the hero, Evelyn, starts out as a man but is changed into a woman (and a beautiful one too, a '*Playboy* centre-fold') by a mad female surgeon – but in my opinion it is a much more effective novel.

The story is narrated in the first person, and it reads like a fever dream. Evelyn is a young Englishman who loves Hollywood movies – particularly the old, black-and-white films of Tristessa de St Ange, '"The Most Beautiful Woman in the World", who executed her symbolic auto-biography in arabesques of kitsch and hyperbole. Tristessa had long since joined Billie Holliday and Judy Garland in the queenly pantheon of women who expose their scars with pride, pointing to their emblematic despair just as a medieval saint points to the wounds of his martyrdom.' The night before he sets out for America, Evelyn watches Tristessa in one of her classic roles, and pays her 'a little tribute of spermatozoa'. On his arrival in New York, he finds himself plunged into a world which is very different from his outdated expectations of that city (based on 1940s movies). There is no suggestion that the novel is set in the future; rather, it deals with a European's dark fantasy of America. For this is the quintessence of 1970s New York: a city of rats and muggers, drug addicts and the muttering insane. It owes more to *Taxi Driver* than *On the Town*.

Black guerrillas are walling off Harlem; tough leather-clad women patrol the streets, harassing all men. 'At the end of July, the sewage system had broken down. The rats grew fat as piglets and vicious as hyenas.' In this corrupt but heady atmosphere, he becomes infatuated with a sexy seventeen-year-old girl. The phantasmagoric scenes in which he first sees her, follows her, and beds her are highly charged with eroticism. In the sour aftermath, when his girlfriend has become pregnant, Evelyn callously decides to abandon her and make his escape from New York. He drives off into the crazy heart of America, in search of emptiness – and himself: 'the world, in time, goes forward and so presents us with the illusion of motion, though all our lives we move through the curvilinear galleries of the brain towards the core of the labyrinth within us.'

His car breaks down in the desert, and he is captured by a tribe of rebel women who carry him to their leader in her underground chambers. This monstrous many-breasted goddess is known to her 'daughters' as Mother, and likes to style herself the Great Parricide or the Grand Emasculator. She goes to work on Evelyn with her surgeon's knife, transforming him into the gorgeous Eve ('she excised everything I had been and left me, instead, with a wound that would, in future, bleed once a month, at the bidding of the moon'). Threatened by impregnation with her own seed, Eve escapes again – only to be captured once more, this time by the drug-created Zero the Poet (the ultimate male chauvinist swine) and his harem of doting wives. Raped and abused by this Charles Manson-like figure, she accompanies him on his mission to raid the home of the retired film actress, Tristessa de St Ange. So Eve is privileged to meet the divine Tristessa at last, and to learn her terrible secret.

First edition: London, Gollancz, 1977 (hardcover)
First American edition: New York, Harcourt Brace Jovanovich, 1977 (hardcover)
Most recent edition: London, Virago (paperback)

63

STEPHEN R. DONALDSON

The Chronicles of Thomas Covenant, the Unbeliever

This mammoth effort, the first published work of its young American author, appeared in three volumes entitled *Lord Foul's Bane*, *The Illearth War* and *The Power That Preserves* (it has been succeeded by three more volumes in *The Second Chronicles*, but I shall not deal with those here). There is no doubt that it belongs to the School of J.R.R. Tolkien. Of all the epic fantasy trilogies which have appeared in the thirty-odd years since *The Lord of the Rings*, Donaldson's has been the most commercially successful, and many readers would argue that it is also the best. It strikes me as being an undeniably impressive, if uneven, work. Donaldson gives us an entire sub-creation – the world of the Land, where the hero (magically displaced from our Earth) embarks on a mighty quest to defeat the corrupting powers of evil as personified by Lord Foul the Despiser. Although the Land bears more than a passing resemblance to Middle-earth, Thomas Covenant himself is a much more modern hero than any of Tolkien's: he is depicted as an *Angst*-ridden solitary who suffers extreme self-doubt – as well as the highly unpleasant physical disease of leprosy. Throughout the three volumes, he is never sure whether or not his experiences in the Land are some sort of terminal delusion, the dream of a sick mind in an ailing body.

As Thomas Covenant travels the Land, eating its medicinal plants, he finds that his body is on the mend: the numbness goes from his fingers and toes as the leprosy abates. However, he is plunged back into the 'real' world at the close of each volume – only to find himself a leper once more. He may grow in moral stature as he learns to take on the responsibilities of a world-saving hero, but there can be no final cure for his physical ailment. A year or so after the trilogy's publication, Donaldson was asked about the message of his huge (and very earnest) fiction. He replied: 'I'll content myself by saying that my conception of "evil" is very much rooted in the real world. I believe that a contempt for life – which manifests itself variously as cynicism, self-pity, self-hatred, racial or sexual prejudice, apathy, environmental suicide, political turpitude, self-righteousness (the list goes on and on) – is the besetting ill of our civilization' (*SF Review*, March 1979). In a lengthy, painful process of learning, Thomas Covenant acquires the courage to fight such evil.

But I regret to say that I am not a Donaldson fan. He is humourless, portentous, elephantine – and his metaphors are often risible ('she raised her head, showing Covenant and Foamfollower the crushed landscape behind her eyes'). His prose is too long-winded, too hamfistedly Latinate, too dependent on a sheer *piling on* effect which reminds me of H.P. Lovecraft's. It is odd that a work which is so difficult to read should have become so popular. Stephen R. Donaldson (born 1947) is the son of an American doctor who ran a leprosarium in India. By making his central figure a leper the author not only creates a powerful metaphor for his hero's alienation, but also gives himself an opportunity to draw on real experience, real pain, of which he presumably has some knowledge. Nevertheless, Donaldson was still a young and impressionable man when he wrote this long novel (he was thirty when it appeared, but it was completed several years before publication): to my mind, it remains a genre exercise – with some interesting and quirky additions. Unlike Tolkien's *The Lord of the Rings*, which I described earlier as the work of a lifetime, *The Chronicles of Thomas Covenant* gives one the sense of being an *unearned* epic.

First edition: New York, Holt, Rinehart & Winston, 1977 (hardcover)
First British edition: London, Fontana, 1978 (paperback)
Most recent edition: New York, Del Rey (paperback)

64

STEPHEN KING

The Shining

King's third published novel was an even greater success than *Carrie* and *'Salem's Lot*, and in some ways it is his most characteristic work. As I have said, he is not an original writer, but in book after book he has shuffled certain standard ingredients with great aplomb. Here we have variations on the haunted house and the magically gifted child, mixed in with the psychological horror of an alcoholic's disintegrating personality. The story was filmed by Stanley Kubrick in 1980, and although the movie has its own icy virtues the scriptwriters made certain crucial changes to the plot which have the effect of robbing the viewer of any sympathy for the tortured central character. It is one of the strengths of King's novel that it does evoke sympathy for all the characters concerned, and particularly for Jack Torrance, the unfortunate hero of the piece.

Torrance is a would-be writer who is suspended from his teaching post as a result of his alcoholism and a violent argument with a student. Swearing off the drink, he accepts a job as winter caretaker at the Overlook Hotel in a lonely part of Colorado. Although warned of a previous caretaker's lapse into murderous insanity, he gladly takes up residence in the deserted mountain-resort hotel with his wife, Wendy, and their five-year-old son, full of determination to write his long-delayed play. They are a loving family, though Torrance is haunted by guilt over the fact that he once broke little Danny's arm when in an alcoholic rage. The boy has long since forgiven him for this and in some ways he feels closer to his father than to his mother. Danny has other reasons for apprehension: unknown to his parents he is gifted with second sight. He can foretell the future, in a limited way, and he is able to hold conversations with his older self (his parents believe 'Tony' to be an imaginary playmate). On their arrival at the huge hotel, which is soon to be snowbound for several months, Danny makes friends with the black cook, Mr Hallorann. The latter also has psychic powers, and can perceive that Danny has 'the shining' – the ability to see things which are invisible to normal eyes. Hallorann warns the boy against entering Room 217 of the hotel (where a ghastly murder was once committed) and drives off for his winter holiday, strangely troubled.

The Torrance family is left alone in the luxurious hotel, and the snow comes down, effectively cutting them off from the outside world. Jack longs for a drink, but takes himself in hand and proceeds with the twin tasks of tending the hotel's ancient heating system and writing his play. Little Danny begins to have terrible dreams, many of which feature the mirror-image word 'REDRUM', and, inevitably, he is tempted to enter Room 217 (his experiences therein constitute the novel's high-point of horror). Meanwhile, Jack discovers some old clippings which reveal the true, bloody history of the hotel. So the narrative wends its lengthy way towards a Grand Guignol finale in which Torrance succumbs to the evil spirits of his environment, and Mr Hallorann rushes to the rescue of mother and son in response to a psychic 'shriek' from the terrified Danny. Despite its occasional predictability, *The Shining* is a gripping story in which the author juggles cleverly with a number of family themes: uxorial and paternal love – and their dark opposites, wife-beating and child-abuse. As in most of King's novels, the characterization, though a touch sentimental, is very effective: a million readers have been moved by these imaginary people, and have seen their own faces in the Gothic mirror of this extravagant fiction.

First edition: New York, Doubleday, 1977 (hardcover)
First British edition: London, New English Library, 1977 (hardcover)
Most recent editions: New York, NAL, and London, NEL (paperbacks)

65

WILLIAM KOTZWINKLE

Fata Morgana

In this pleasing confection of a novel everything is done by mirrors. Or rather, it is done by mesmerism, Tarot cards, crystal balls and clockwork. *Fata Morgana* is a mock nineteenth-century entertainment, in part a pastiche of those early French detective stories of the Émile Gaboriau type. Like Gaboriau's eminent Monsieur Lecoq, Kotzwinkle's tough middle-aged hero, Inspector Paul Picard, is a member of the Paris Sûreté. The year is 1861, and Picard is on the trail of one Ric Lazare, a fortune-telling magician who apparently makes his living by swindling the rich and fashionable set. Disguised as a pearl dealer, Picard visits Lazare's salon, where he is overcome by the voluptuous beauty of the mysterious Madame Renée Lazare – 'she touched her hand to the chain of velvet flowers in her hair, and Picard felt velvet petals opening in his stomach as she glanced toward him. The sensation was unbearably delicious.' Lazare himself claims to be over five thousand years old, a master of ancient mysteries. Whatever the truth, he makes a fool of the detective by swiftly seeing through Picard's disguise. In desperation, the policeman leaves Paris in search of some evidence which will condemn Lazare.

There follows a bizarrely dream-like hunt through middle Europe. Picard seeks for traces of Ric and Renée Lazare in Vienna, and seems to find a clue among an exhibition of clockwork toys at a fairground booth. This leads him north to a small German city, where he looks for the craftsman who made these ingenious automata and to whom Ric Lazare was once apprenticed. Thence Picard travels to the aptly-named Valley of Deep Sorrow in a remote part of Hungary, and thence to Transylvania, still in pursuit of the truth about the elusive Lazare and his beautiful, unattainable wife. One of his informants warns him: 'A mirage, Inspector. The fabulous Fata Morgana. Only the peasants let the mirage rule their life, daydreaming over it.' Picard returns to Paris, his head reeling with the notion that Lazare is in fact the long-lived Count Cagliostro (a real-life eighteenth-century magician and adventurer). There he confronts his devious quarry once more, and is nearly seduced by the gorgeous Renée.

This is a deceptive story of illusion and reality, full of period detail, richly written and highly erotic. It is an enjoyable literary exercise, perhaps lacking in any final significance but certainly a *tour de force*. William Kotzwinkle (born 1938) is the American author of *Swimmer in the Secret Sea* (1975), *Doctor Rat* (1976; a winner of the World Fantasy Award) and other fabulations. He has also written numerous children's books, and is now best known for his novelization of Steven Spielberg's film *E.T.: The Extra-Terrestrial* (1982) and its sequel *E.T.: The Book of the Green Planet* (1985). Kotzwinkle is a writer of many parts.

First edition: New York, Knopf, 1977 (hardcover)
First British edition: London, Hutchinson, 1977 (hardcover)
Most recent editions: New York, Bantam, and London, Black Swan (paperbacks)

66

FRITZ LEIBER

Our Lady of Darkness

There have been countless tales of haunted houses – old buildings, ranging from medieval castles to twentieth-century hotels, plagued by ghosts, spirits, poltergeists, what-have-you. In Leiber's ingenious variation on the theme, the ghostly beings are known as 'paramental entities', and it is not just one building but a whole city (present-day San Francisco) which is haunted by them. Moreover, in a clever and elegant switch on our expectations, this book's hero is able to tell that his own home is haunted only when he views it through binoculars from a distance of two miles.

Franz Westen is a middle-aged writer of horror fiction who lives, surrounded by his books and magazines, in a San Francisco apartment block. He is recovering from a long alcoholic binge which followed on the premature death of his wife, and he has been enjoying an on/off relationship with a young woman musician who lives two floors down from him. Franz is in the process of rediscovering ordinary life, and he takes a particular pleasure in gazing at the stars and the city through his binoculars. One morning he examines Corona Heights, a steep hill which rises from the streets a couple of miles away, and he notices a pale brown figure dancing eccentrically at its summit. He decides to go for a walk, and to investigate Corona Heights. When he arrives there the mysterious figure has gone. From the hilltop Franz searches for his own apartment window, catches sight of it through the lenses, and is horrified to see *a pale brown creature leaning from the window and waving back at him*. An old folk-rhyme runs through his mind: 'I went to Taffy's house, Taffy wasn't home. Taffy went to my house and stole a marrowbone.'

It is a chilling moment, and things develop spookily from there. Franz discovers that his apartment building was once a hotel, where lived an eccentric scholar of the supernatural named Thibaut de Castries. He already owns a rare book by de Castries, entitled *Megapolisomancy: A New Science of Cities*. He now reads this apparently crack-brained work of pseudo-science with renewed interest, and it begins to make a strange kind of sense. De Castries believed that modern cities, with their vast quantities of steel, concrete, oil, paper, and electrical energy were breeding grounds for so-called paramental entities – which is to say, ghosts befitting a technological era. It would seem that a supernatural line of power runs between Corona Heights and the apartment block (which was once a hotel where de Castries himself resided): Franz Westen is being haunted by a paramental.

The novel contains a great deal of talk – but it is fascinating talk, for most of Leiber's people are a pleasure to meet. Despite a lack of action in the middle passages, the climax of the story is truly frightening. The bookish Franz encounters a nightmarish 'Lady of Darkness' who draws her sustenance from raw materials which are very dear to his heart. At the end, he comes close to the point of dissolution, but survives. *Our Lady of Darkness* is a first-class supernatural horror story, written with all the relaxed ease of an old master. It is plainly an autobiographical fantasy, one which speaks of real suffering, but it also has a mellow quality.

First edition: New York, Putnam, 1977 (hardcover)
First British edition: London, Millington, 1978 (hardcover)
Most recent edition: New York, Ace (paperback)

67

MICHAEL MOORCOCK

Gloriana, or The Unfulfill'd Queen

'While it is neither an "Elizabethan Fantasia," nor an historical novel, this romance does have some relation to the Faerie Queen,' states Michael Moorcock in an author's note. Even more obvious is the debt which this amazing novel owes to Mervyn Peake, not least in its opening description of Queen Gloriana's colossal palace (shades of Gormenghast):

> The palace is as large as a good-sized town, for through the centuries its outbuildings, its lodges, its guest houses, the mansions of its lords and ladies in waiting, have been linked by covered ways, and those covered ways roofed, in turn, so that here and there we find corridors within corridors, like conduits in a tunnel, houses within rooms, those rooms within castles, those castles within artificial caverns, the whole roofed again with tiles of gold and platinum and silver, marble and mother-of-pearl, so that the palace glares with a thousand colours in the sunlight, shimmers constantly in the moonlight, its walls appearing to undulate, its roofs to rise and fall like a glamorous tide, its towers and minarets lifting like the masts and hulks of sinking ships.

Gloriana's labyrinthine home, bequeathed to her by her insane father, King Hern, is the setting for most of the story. Its walls conceal endless secrets. Beggars and madmen spy on the rich and powerful in their sumptuous apartments; there are hidden seraglios and oubliettes, rooms given over to every imaginable vice, visible only to the rat-like watchers in the walls. This age-old structure is like the model of a well-stocked but deteriorating brain; it is the essence of all palaces, all castles, and the most extravagant such creation in the whole of fiction.

The place is London, capital of the realm of Albion, and leading city of a huge overseas empire (which includes a North America called, logically enough, 'Virginia'). The customs and technologies of the society are Elizabethan, but this is not an alternative-history novel in the strict sense: there is no fixed point at which Albion's history diverged from our own. Like Gormenghast or Malacia, Gloriana's London stands outside time, a never-world which resembles the ideal (and the nightmare) of some sixteenth-century dreamer. The Queen's reign is hailed as a golden age, with the tall, beautiful Gloriana as a paragon of virtue; but there is a frankly acknowledged darker side to things, a murky obverse to all the splendour and the poetry. Albion's power is maintained by unscrupulous agents, chief among them the turncoat Captain Quire whose treachery precipitates much of the story's action. And Gloriana herself, although at first ignorant of all these political machinations, is racked by a dreadful, symbolic sexual need. Her nights are made feverish by desires which cannot be sated: she is, after all, the 'unfulfill'd queen'. In order for her to find fulfilment, and for a true golden age to dawn, it is necessary that some kind of balance be achieved – an intelligent compromise between idealism and cynicism.

Gloriana is a long novel: copiously inventive, funny, exciting, sometimes disgusting, and always rich with allusions. It contains references not only to Spenser, Peake and English history, but to the whole of Michael Moorcock's own extensive body of fiction – from Sexton Blake and Elric of Melniboné (*30*) to Una Persson and the Dancers at the End of Time. Although brilliantly successful in its own terms, it is also a portmanteau work which serves as a keystone in a personal mythology: a summing-up of the fifty or so novels which its author had already produced, and a clearing of the decks in preparation for other major books to come.

First edition: London, Allison & Busby, 1978 (hardcover)
First American edition: New York, Avon, 1979 (paperback)
Most recent editions: London, Fontana, and New York, Popular Library (paperbacks)

68

J.G. BALLARD

The Unlimited Dream Company

This novel by the grand master of modern British science fiction came as a surprise. Unlike his previous full-length works, it is an out-and-out fantasy, a tale of magical transformations, of mysticism and flight. Set in the present day, in Ballard's home town of Shepperton, Middlesex, it is a magnificent rhapsody on the absurd ambitions of the Self, and it is (in Anthony Burgess's words, quoted on the jacket of the first edition) 'as basic as a dream of the whole human race'.

The narrator, a 25-year-old misfit called Blake, crashes his stolen aircraft into the River Thames. He apparently dies and is reborn as 'a minor deity'. Quickened by strange powers, he finds himself unable to leave the riverside town of Shepperton and he begins to remould the lives of its inhabitants. There is some suggestion that this is all a split-second fantasy in the dying brain of the illicit aviator (compare William Golding's *Pincher Martin*), but Ballard does not drive home any 'rational' explanation. The situation allows the author to give full rein to his tremendous inventive powers.

Sleepy humdrum Shepperton is remade by Blake as a jungle town, filled with colourful plants, birds and animals. In some of the most effective passages, the hero enters into the consciousness of various creatures, learning how to fly like a condor, swim like a dolphin, run like a deer:

> I sailed grandly through the cold air. I could see my huge wings and the fluted rows of ice-white feathers, and feel

the powerful muscles across my chest. I raked the sky with the claws of a great raptor. A coarse plumage encased me, reeking with an acrid odour that was not the scent of a mammal. I tasted the foul spoor-lines that tainted the night air. I was no graceful aerial being, but a condor of violent energy, my cloaca encrusted with excrement and semen. I was ready to mate with the wind.

Later, Blake teaches the townsfolk to fly, absorbing them into his own body then expelling them once more. Eventually he learns a kind of humility and gives himself away, piece by piece, to the town's inhabitants. But there is a continual dark undertone: love and hate merge and become indistinguishable, giving of oneself becomes the ultimate selfishness. This is a novel full of Ballardian imagery, wonder and menace. It is also wayward, paradoxical, and baffling. Not the least of its appeals is the undercurrent of black humour, exemplified by the central notion of a suburban Dionysus, a dying god for the contemporary Home Counties. *The Unlimited Dream Company* may also be read as a 'secret autobiography', a fable about the artist's relationship with his dull, bourgeois neighbours.

James Graham Ballard (born 1930) has transcended the science fiction field, where he began his career as a contributor to *New Worlds* and other magazines. He is now regarded as a leading imaginative novelist, one who has successfully imported a brand of surrealism into English fiction. His work is always startlingly clear and explicit – as well-lit, as unmistakable and as haunting as the paintings of Salvador Dali. *The Unlimited Dream Company* is one of his finest novels.

First edition: London, Cape, 1979 (hardcover)
First American edition: New York, Holt, Rinehart & Winston, 1979 (hardcover)
Most recent editions: London, Granada, and New York, Pocket Books (paperbacks)

69

PHYLLIS EISENSTEIN

Sorcerer's Son

It is refreshing to come across a high fantasy novel which begins with 'Chapter One' – and launches you straight into the story. There is no prefatory matter here, and there are no appendages: no maps, genealogies, lists of dramatis personae, or glossaries. Although it is a longish novel of almost 400 pages, there are no divisions into 'Parts' or 'Books', no chapter titles, no epigraphs. In short, there is no cumbersome apparatus whatsoever – just a good, plain tale written in pellucid style. Phyllis Eisenstein (born 1946) is an American author who has produced both science fiction and fantasy, though not a great deal of either, and this is probably her best book.

The setting is vaguely medieval and wooded, the society feudal and chivalric (as in Patricia McKillip's *The Forgotten Beasts of Eld*, the social background is sketchy, and some readers may find this an irritating lack; others may find it a pleasingly bare set for the all-important drama of love, magic and Oedipal conflict). Here the sorceress Delivev lives alone in Castle Spinweb. Her power resides in her magical ability to manipulate all things woven – ranging from human-made fabrics to spider's webs. She is able to view far scenes with the help of her gossamer webs, and even to listen to distant troubadours' songs through the medium of her tiny spider 'spies'. She is content to live alone and believes she has no enemies. However, one of Delivev's fellow sorcerers – Rezhyk, a summoner of demons – feels threatened by her (after all, she has the means to make one of his own shirts strangle him). He offers his hand in marriage, and is rebuffed. In pique, he summons a demon, Gildrum, and commands it to take attractive human form in order to seduce the sorceress – for pregnancy will temporarily dampen her magical powers and enable him to prepare defences. Accordingly, Gildrum arrives at Castle Spinweb in the shape of a sorely-wounded but handsome young knight. Delivev gladly takes him in, tends his injury, and allows him to dally for some weeks. She duly falls in love, and is heartbroken when he leaves ('a woman wailing for a demon lover,' as the cover blurb aptly, but perhaps too melodramatically, informs us).

The fruit of her loins (and the demon's seed) is a baby whom she names Cray. He swiftly grows to be a strapping lad whose dearest wish is to be a knight errant, just like his long-lost father. His mother tries to dissuade him, but as soon as he is able he leaves home. The bulk of the novel is a picaresque account of the teenage Cray's adventures as he searches for his father, protected by his mother's spiders, and hindered along the way by the evil machinations of the paranoid sorcerer Rezhyk. He acquires a companion, who plays Sancho to Cray's extremely young Don Quixote, and gradually he learns the ways of the world. At length, he heeds his mother's advice and turns to sorcery as the only means to unravel the mystery of his parentage. He too learns how to summon demons:

> They did come in their own good time – spheres of liquid large as bears, milky, opalescent; and giant snow-flakes like stars made of glittering openwork lace, with needle-sharp spicules sprouting in every direction. And not only ice and water demons came, but fire as well, blobs of flame from candle-lights to roaring conflagrations. Cray would hardly look up from his books, without seeing some unhuman being floating in the blue, glowing by its own light or reflecting the luminosity of Air from a pearl-smooth or crystalline surface.

With the help of these free beings, he defeats the evil sorcerer – and becomes reconciled with the demon Gildrum, his 'father'.

First edition: New York, Del Rey, 1979 (paperback)

70

JONATHAN CARROLL

The Land of Laughs

This enjoyable fantasy-mystery story by an American writer (born 1945) has been described by Stanislaw Lem, the distinguished Polish novelist, as 'a great *tour de force*'. It is certainly an original and curious book, with a strong flavour which is all its own. The narrative concerns the uncanny events which occur when Thomas Abbey and his girlfriend Saxony Gardner visit the small town of Galen, Missouri, in order to research a biography of their favourite author of children's books. The late, great Marshall France, whose novels for young readers include such whimsical titles as *The Green Dog's Sorrow*, *The Pool of Stars* and *The Land of Laughs*, led an extremely reclusive life in Galen, where he died at the age of 44 (some years before this story begins). Thomas and Saxony are avid fans of Marshall France's work, having been haunted all their lives by his magical prose, his talking animals and his eccentric but lovable human characters. However, little is known about the writer; and Thomas, who is unhappy in his work as a schoolteacher, decides to take a year's sabbatical in order to produce a biography – with Saxony's help.

Neither of them has pursued writing as a hobby – Thomas is a keen collector of old masks, and Saxony makes hand-carved marionettes – but they are confident that their love for Marshall France's creations will carry them through their self-imposed task. On arriving in the midwestern town, they meet France's daughter, Anna, a beautiful woman in her mid-thirties. They have been led to believe by France's publisher that Anna will prove difficult and obstructive (a previous would-be biographer of her father was given a very frosty reception) but, on the contrary, they are pleased to discover that Anna and the rest of the townsfolk are all exceedingly co-operative. They soon find comfortable lodgings, and Anna invites them to dinner at her house:

> In the incredible France living room my first amazed inventory took in: a hand-carved olive-wood Pinocchio with moving arms and legs, six-foot tall department store mannequin from the 1920s that was painted silver and looked like Jean Harlow with her hair swept up on her head, Navaho rug. Hand puppets and marionettes. *Masks!* (Mostly Japanese, South American, and African on first glance.) Peacock feathers stuck in an earthenware pitcher. Japanese prints (Hokusai and Hiroshige). A shelf full of old alarm clocks with painted faces, metal banks, and tin toys. Old leather-bound books.
>
> We stood in the doorway and gasped. He wrote the books, and this was his living room, and it all made perfect sense.

The imagery of toys, puppets, mannequins and masks also makes sense in the context of the novel, for it begins to emerge that there is something curiously *unreal* – something artificially contrived and perhaps even sinister – about the town of Galen and its inhabitants.

Numerous small details add to a growing atmosphere of unease, although nothing overtly fantastic happens until some two-thirds of the way through the novel. Then Thomas hears a dog *talking* in its sleep: it has a high-pitched, nearly human voice – like an imaginary beast from one of Marshall France's books. From this point on Thomas has a terrible conviction that he and Saxony have somehow strayed into a world created by their favourite author. But it would be remiss of me to give away more of the story's development here. *The Land of Laughs* is an effective chiller which depends on its surprises.

First edition: New York, Viking, 1980 (hardcover)
First British edition: London, Hamlyn, 1982 (paperback)
Most recent editions: New York, Ace, and London, Arrow (paperbacks)

71

SUZY McKEE CHARNAS

The Vampire Tapestry

Peter S. Beagle describes this clever book as the best vampire novel he has ever read, and I would concur with his judgement. It consists of five linked stories about a present-day vampire who calls himself Dr Edward L. Weyland, PhD. He drinks blood, and is immensely long-lived, but in every other respect he seems a normal, suffering member of the human race. A predator who rarely kills, he is also an accomplished intellectual, an anthropologist who writes books and gives fascinating lectures. For the most part, we see him through others' eyes, and Suzy McKee Charnas's peculiar achievement is to have produced a 'vampire novel' which is more concerned with the variety of human responses to the monster than with the monster himself. Written in a spare, hard-edged style (touched with humour), it is a much more sophisticated book than other latter-day tales of the undead (such as Stephen King's *'Salem's Lot*, or Anne Rice's *Interview with the Vampire*), and yet it is also a gripping read. It deserves to be better known.

At one point Dr Weyland is captured by some petty hoodlums who intend to exploit him as a freak attraction in an illicit sideshow. They have to feed their captive, however, and among the 'volunteers' who give their blood is a young woman called Bobbie:

> 'Oh,' she said softly. And then, still staring, 'Oh, wow. Oh, Wesley, he's drinking my blood.'
> She put out her hand as if to push the vampire's head

away, but instead she began to stroke his hair. She murmured, 'I read my tarot this morning and I could see there would be fantastic new things, and I should get right behind them and be real positive, you know?' Until he finished she sat enthralled, whispering 'Oh, wow,' at dreamy intervals.

When the vampire lifted his drowned, peaceful face, she said earnestly to him, 'I'm a Scorpio; what's your sign?'

Although he is more interested in survival than sex, Weyland has this sort of effect on many of the women he meets. The novel's central episode concerns his relationship with a female psychotherapist who gradually comes to love him. At first she is convinced that he is suffering from psychotic delusions, and she sets out to 'cure' him. In time, however, she realizes that he is a true vampire – the last member of an alien race, an archetypal loner, one who must for ever elude the 'peasants with torches' who threaten his existence. Weyland demands nothing of human beings, except their blood, yet his respect for this unusual woman grows and eventually he is able to return her love. Their tryst is brief, for in order to function in this world he must leave her and take up a new identity elsewhere.

Weyland meets all types, ranging from the lady psychotherapist through the feather-brained Bobbie and an insecure fourteen-year-old boy, to sundry inadequate academics and a self-styled 'Satanist' – this last is a vain, bombastic villain who acts as a cynical Van Helsing to Weyland's oddly noble Dracula. Given the premise of a blood-drinking immortal protagonist, the story is developed in thoroughly realistic terms. There are no bats or garlic, crucifixes or wooden stakes here. Instead we have a credible range of skilfully depicted human foibles. Suzy McKee Charnas (born 1939) has breathed new life into the vampire legend, rescuing her hero from the horror-movie clichés and giving him a fresh status as a darkly romantic outsider.

First edition: New York, Simon & Schuster, 1980 (hardcover)
First British edition: London, Granada, 1983 (paperback)
Most recent edition: New York, Tor (paperback)

72

M. JOHN HARRISON

A Storm of Wings

The first edition of this remarkably stylish fantasy was subtitled: 'Being the second volume of the "Viriconium" sequence, in which Benedict Paucemanly returns from his long frozen dream in the far side of the Moon, and the Earth submits briefly to the charisma of the Locust.' One part Mervyn Peake, another part Jack Vance, and a third part the product of Harrison's own unique sensibility, it is the middle volume of what the author chooses to call his 'Viriconium sequence'. The three novels of the said sequence do not constitute a trilogy in the normal sense of the term, for they are all very different. *The Pastel City* (1971), an adventure story of the distant future, was a colourful exercise in the packing-in of action: a sword-and-sorcery potboiler by a highly talented new writer. The third book, *In Viriconium* (1982), is slimmer, harder and sparer then the preceding two. This last volume is not futuristic in the least: Viriconium, although a city in some alternative dimension, has all the grittiness of a present-day London or Manchester. By contrast, *A Storm of Wings*, the book I have chosen to highlight here, is a lush and involuted fantasy of far-future decadence.

Above all, it is a triumph of style. We are in the Evening of the world, long after the technical brilliance of the Afternoon Cultures has rusted away, and never has a 'Dying Earth' setting been more intensely evoked:

Cellur the Bird Lord: he has lived for aeons in a five-sided tower full of undersea gloaming. Instruments flickered and ticked about him all that time, while his sensors licked the unquiet air, detecting new forms and seasons. Out of the cold reaches of salt marsh and estuary, out of the long cry of the wind, out of the swell of the sea and the call of the winter tern he comes to us now: out of the War of the Two Queens, with his thousand dying metal birds; out of the long forgotten dream of the Middle Period of the Earth . . .

The lines and figures on his marvellous robe writhe and shiver like tortured alien animals. Geometry remembers, though he may not. 'Nothing is left as it was,' they sigh, 'in that final perfect world. The towers that ruled these wastes have fallen now. Their libraries lie open like the pages of a book abandoned to the desert wind, their last dry whispers fade; philosophers and clowns alike, fade.'

Of course, this kind of thing has been done before, by Vance among others, but in Harrison's case such romantic mood-setting is tempered by his excellent knowledge of geology and topography (his wastelands are depicted with a seasoned fell-walker's eye) and by his sharp awareness of human vanities and moral failings: no supermen swagger across these entropic landscapes.

The principal characters are a motley gang of reluctant adventurers (most of them revenants from *The Pastel City*, now grown old). In addition to Cellur the Bird Lord, we meet Alstath Fulthor, first of the Reborn Men; Galen Hornwrack, a sour mercenary; and Tomb the Iron Dwarf, most endearing of the story's people – a tough, tinker-like scavenger of ancient technologies who feels obliged to remind himself from time to time that he is 'a dwarf and not a philosopher'. Together, they embark on a quest to discover the meaning of all the sinister insectile portents which have been troubling the city of Viriconium. They are assisted by a madwoman who brings them the head of a giant locust, and by the overweight ghost of the aforementioned Benedict Paucemanly, an 'airboatman' who once flew to the Moon and came back with more than he bargained for. Around these comical characters and their decaying world M. John Harrison (born 1945) has spun an amazing web of poetry.

First edition: New York, Doubleday, 1980 (hardcover)
First British edition: London, Sphere Books, 1980 (paperback)
Most recent edition: London, Unwin (paperback)

73

RUDY RUCKER

White Light, or
What is Cantor's Continuum Problem?

Rucker's highly original and amusing book was published as science fiction (mathematical sf, a rare sub-genre) but it is in fact a supernatural fantasy. The author himself uses the term 'transrealism', which can mean what you will. His hero and narrator, Felix Rayman, is a young college lecturer who has a taste for abstruse mathematics and heavy rock music. Alienated by his all-too-straight surroundings, he experiments with lucid dream-states, and this leads him on to out-of-body experiences – 'during the lucid dreaming my spirit had gotten used to moving about Dreamland in a self-generated astral body'. One day, while mulling over Georg Cantor's continuum problem and the riddle of infinity, Felix falls asleep in a graveyard and subsequently finds that he is unable to re-enter his old body:

> At a touch of volition my astral body floated over to my inert flesh. The body was lying supine near the base of the beech tree. The rain came down through the bare branches to split into droplets on the greasy face. Fortunately the head was twisted to the side, and the water couldn't fill the crooked nostrils or the slack mouth. The body looked utterly uninviting, but I began to try to get back into it.
>
> I had never been out so long before. My astral body had flowed into a blobbier, more comfortable shape, which was hard to fit to my old skeleton. The space occupied by my flesh had a clammy, icky feel to it. It

was like the body cavity of a defrosted turkey, full of pimply skin, splintery bones, and slippery giblets.

He is forced to give up the attempt to shuffle on those mortal coils. These strange (but somehow unthreatening) experiences culminate in a lengthy trip through the afterlife in search of an elusive realm known as Cimön. Felix zooms through space with the greatest of ease: 'the thousand light-year trip across the galaxy only seemed to take half an hour.' Along the way he is privileged to meet Jesus Christ and the Devil, as well as his favourite trio of great mathematicians, Cantor, Hilbert and Einstein, among many others. Arriving in Cimön, he soon finds himself checking into an infinite hotel, climbing an infinite mountain and wandering in an infinite library – in pursuit of the white light, God, and the answer to Cantor's continuum problem.

Funny, flippant and staggeringly inventive, *White Light* is a delightful *Alice in Wonderland* for our times, packed with incident and paradox and grotesque characters (one of Felix's principal guides is a gigantic beetle called Franx). The story may be a little too fast-moving and flippant for some, but the secret of the book's appeal lies principally in its *tone*, an effervescent blending of heavy mathematics with a hippie sensibility. Rudolf von Bitter Rucker (born 1946) claims to be the great-great-great grandson of the German philosopher Hegel. A sometime Associate Professor of mathematics at various American colleges, he has written several popular maths books (with titles like *Geometry, Relativity and the Fourth Dimension*, 1977) as well as science fiction and fantasy novels such as *White Light, Software* (1982) and *The Secret of Life* (1985). As a writer of fiction, Rucker is a cherishable eccentric – one of the wild men of the modern imagination.

First edition: London, Virgin Books, 1980 (paperback)
First American edition: New York, Ace, 1980 (paperback)

74

CHELSEA QUINN YARBRO

Ariosto

I admire thoroughly researched historical fiction but by and large I have no great fondness for so-called historical fantasy, whether of the genre type produced by, say, Katherine Kurtz in her 'Deryni' books, or of the mainstream sort written by novelists as distinguished as Norman Mailer (*Ancient Evenings*, 1983) and Joseph Heller (*God Knows*, 1984). Whatever their particular merits, such works are neither fish nor fowl. But I reserve the right to be inconsistent: Swann's *Day of the Minotaur*, Davidson's *The Phoenix and the Mirror* and Moorcock's *Gloriana* are pleasing exceptions, novels in which the fantasy counts for more than the history – and Yarbro's *Ariosto* is another such.

The book is subtitled 'Ariosto Furioso, a Romance for an Alternate Renaissance.' The hero is Lodovico Ariosto, author of *Orlando Furioso* (1516–32), a 46-canto epic poem which ranks as one of the great European works of fantasy. Orlando (the Italian version of Charlemagne's paladin Roland) encounters an enchanted castle, a flying horse, a hippogriff and many other marvels – and even flies to the moon in the prophet Elijah's chariot. Some of the magic of Ariosto's wondrous verse narrative is sought for and found by the American writer Chelsea Quinn Yarbro (born 1942) in this, perhaps the best of her several historical fantasies. (Her other works include the well-received *Hotel Transylvania* [1978] – a vampire novel with an eighteenth-century French setting – and its four or five sequels.)

The narrative consists of two parallel strands, which are presented to us in alternating chapters headed 'La Fantasia' and 'La Realtà'. The events of these strands gradually converge and come together in a brief final episode. In the 'fantasy' chapters we are clearly in the world of Ariosto's dreams. The setting is a North America, the land of the Cérocchi Indians, which has been successfully colonized by the federated states of Italy. To this romantic land comes the gallant Ariosto on his flying steed – no mere poet but a warrior prince who will assist the colonists and their Indian allies in a mighty struggle against the Fortezza Serpente, the supernatural powers of darkness. In the 'reality' chapters we are in the city of Florence in the year 1533, where the middle-aged, short-sighted Ariosto serves as court poet to 'il Primàrio', the man who is king in all but name. But this Machiavellian setting does not quite belong to the history we know – for we are in a time-line where the greatest of the Medicis, Lorenzo the Magnificent, did not die at the age of forty-three but instead lived on into his seventies, engineering a more-or-less harmonious Italian Federation and a peace treaty with the Turks. These developments have opened up the very real possibility of Italian participation in the exploration of the New World (we must remember that Columbus was Genoese, and it was only as a result of historical 'accident' that he discovered America on behalf of the King of Spain). Il Primàrio of the novel is Lorenzo de' Medici's grandson, Damanio, and it is this cunning but idealistic leader whom Ariosto is imagined as serving. Like his grandfather, Damiano is an enlightened patron of the arts as well as a skilful politician. Thus the poet's attractive 'fantasia' is rooted in the 'realtà' of his times.

We have the novelist's vision of a better world, within which nests another vision of a world better still. Sadly, both visions turn out to be fleeting, for a harsh politics comes to prevail in Florence, and even Ariosto's dream of a utopian America begins to go sour. But there is much excitement and enchantment along the way in this satisfying complex novel about history and desire.

First edition: New York, Pocket Books, 1980 (paperback)
Most recent edition: New York, Tor (paperback)

75

WILLIAM S. BURROUGHS

Cities of the Red Night

Cities was received as Burroughs's most significant book since *The Naked Lunch* (1959). It was described as some kind of masterpiece by critics as various as Peter Ackroyd, Christopher Isherwood and Ken Kesey. This may have been due to the fact that it was his most straightforward and 'linear' narrative to date, less fragmentary than such works as *Nova Express* (1964) and *The Wild Boys* (1971). Nevertheless, it is still a novel of disparate parts: strands of story interweave, each surging into prominence then fading away, without any clear beginning, middle and ending to the whole. But one does not expect the conventional from William Burroughs (born 1914): he is one of those who 'transmit their reports at midnight from the dark causeways of our own spinal columns' (in J.G. Ballard's memorable words). In some respects he is the greatest fantasist of the second half of the twentieth century, the cartographer of our most horrible nightmares.

The cities of the title are called Tamaghis, Ba'dan, Yass-Waddah, Waghdas, Naufana and Ghadis. Once centres of civilization and learning, they are imagined as existing a hundred millennia ago in the area which is now the Gobi Desert. A cosmic catastrophe turns the sky red and causes genetic mutations. Up until now all people have been black, but red, yellow and white skins begin to appear for the first time, and civil strife ensues: 'The women, led by an albino mutant known as the White Tigress, seized Yass-Waddah, reducing the male inhabitants to slaves . . . The

Council in Waghdas countered by developing a method of growing babies in excised wombs . . . Many strange mutants arose as a series of plagues devastated the cities . . . Finally, the cities were abandoned and the survivors fled in all directions, carrying the plagues with them.' But these cities do not exist merely in historical fantasy: they are symbolic places, to be visited in dreams – and possibly they still endure, except that now they have names like New York, London, Moscow, Tokyo, Paris, Shanghai.

The vivid scraps of narrative leap from past to present to future: 'Ba'dan is the oldest spaceport on planet Earth and like many port towns has accreted over the centuries the worst features of many times and places. Riffraff and misfits from every corner of the galaxy have jumped ship here or emigrated to engage in various pernicious and parasitic occupations.' Intermingled with the parable of the cities are an eighteenth-century story of boy pirates who fight the Spanish and attempt to found a womanless utopia; a present-day tale of a private eye, Clem Snide, who investigates murder and is drawn into the contemplation of ancient mysteries; a 1920s story about the travels of Farnsworth, a stiff-upper-lipped District Health Officer and not-so-secret drug addict; and more, in parodic, menacing or elegiac veins.

Characters recur from earlier Burroughs books, as do the usual obsessions with drugs, death by hanging, and homosexuality. The imagery is both haunting – 'Smell of the salt marshes, slivers of ice at dawn, catwalks, towers, and wooden houses over the water where white-furred crocodiles lurk . . .' – and wildly, grossly funny: 'The subtlest assassins among them are the Dream Killers or Bangutot Boys. They have the ability to invade the REM sleep of the target, fashion themselves from the victim's erection, and grow from his sexual energy until they are solid enough to strangle him.' In the end, after all the revels are ended, the author seems to speak in his own voice: 'I have blown a hole in time with a firecracker. Let others step through . . . A nightmare feeling of foreboding and desolation comes over me as a great mushroom-shaped cloud darkens the earth. A few may get through the gate in time.'

First edition: London, Calder, 1981 (hardcover)
First American edition: New York, Holt, Rinehart &
Winston, 1981 (hardcover)
Most recent editions: London, Picador, and New York, Holt
(paperbacks)

76

JOHN CROWLEY

Little, Big

The title is open to many readings: the Little and the Big
are the country and the city, the inside and the outside, the
private and the public, the faerie and the human. And much
more. The author's intended subtitle was consigned by the
publishers to the contents page: there we learn that the
work is really called *Little, Big; or, The Fairies' Parliament*.
It is indeed about fairies and fairyland, as well as being a
family saga and a multiple love story. It is also perhaps 'the
greatest fantasy novel ever' (in Thomas M. Disch's words)
and 'a book that all by itself calls for a redefinition of
fantasy' (according to Ursula Le Guin). A novel of architec-
tonic sublimity, *Little, Big* beggars the words of criticism.

The central character is a young city-dweller called
Smoky Barnable, who falls in love with a country girl
named Daily Alice Drinkwater. Leaving his dull job in the
city, Smoky hikes to Edgewood, the Drinkwaters' rural
New England home. And there he finds magic, quite
literally. Edgewood is a comfortable folly, built by Daily
Alice's great-grandfather who was the author of a nineteenth-century text on country houses: it is a 'compound
illustration of the plates of his famous book – several
different houses of different sizes and styles collapsed
together'. Near this remarkable dwelling are woods which
seem to be inhabited by tiny folk who are visible only from
the corner of the eye. After an outdoor wedding, Smoky
and Daily Alice go for a woodland honeymoon, and the
landscape is in sympathy with their emotions: 'he thought
he had never looked into anywhere so deeply and secretly

211

The Wood as this. For some reason its floor was carpeted with moss, not thick with the irregulars of the forest's edge, shrub and briar and small aspen. It led inward, it drew them inward into whispering darkness.'

Crowley evokes his fairyland with consummate delicacy: nothing is crassly asserted, little is brought into the full day-light, but an infinite variety of wonders is obliquely suggested. The reader trembles on the brink of successive revelations, as the author plays with masterly skill on the emotional nerves of awe, rapture, mystery and enchantment. In one of the novel's many historical flashbacks we meet Dr Bramble, one of Daily Alice's forefathers, and we listen to his comically pedantic (but wise) lecture on the fairy folk:

'Nereids, dryads, sylphs and salamanders is how Paracelsus divides them,' Dr Bramble said. 'That is to say (as we would express it) mermaids, elves, fairies, and goblins or imps. One class of spirit for each of the four elements – mermaids for the water, elves for the earth, fairies for the air, goblins for the fire . . .

'These elementals . . . can be any of several different sizes and (as we might put it) densities . . . In their sylphlike or pixie manifestation they appear no bigger than a large insect, or a hummingbird; they are said to inhabit the woods, they are associated with flowers. In other instances, they appear to be a foot to three feet in height, wingless, fully formed little men and women . . . And there are fairy warriors on great steeds, banshees and pookahs and ogres who are huge, larger by far than men . . .

'The explanation is that the world inhabited by these beings is . . . another world entirely, and it is enclosed within this one, with a peculiar geography I can only describe as *infundibular*.' He paused for effect. 'I mean by this that the other world is composed of a series of concentric rings, which as one penetrates deeper into the other world, grow larger. The further in you go, the bigger it gets.'

Which is a beautiful analogy for this novel by John Crowley (born 1942). It is a long, slow, pastoral tale that moves from past to future and involves a host of vivid characters. The more it ensnares our eager imaginations, the bigger it seems to become.

First edition: New York, Bantam, 1981 (paperback)
First British edition: London, Gollancz, 1982 (hardcover)
Most recent edition: New York, Bantam, and London, Methuen (paperbacks)

77

ALASDAIR GRAY

Lanark: A Life in Four Books

This is another big novel – a lifetime's work, really, since small parts of it first appeared as short stories in the 1950s and 1960s. Alasdair Gray (born 1934), artist and playwright, is a Glaswegian Scot, and *Lanark*, his first novel, has already been hailed as a Scottish epic of sorts. Written with all the fresh energy of an idealistic autodidact, the book has been described by its author as an 'exaggerated spiritual autobiography, a daft *Divine Comedy*'; it is also, in Anthony Burgess's words, 'a shattering work of fiction in the modern idiom'. Gray's idiom may be modern, but it embraces many traditional things; not only autobiographical realism, but low comedy, afterlife fantasy, scattershot satire, nightmarish allegory, self-referential metafiction, tender eroticism, lunatic scholarship and profuse literary borrowings.

Divided into four 'Books', *Lanark* is a novel with two heroes, and two major settings. About half of the narrative is realistic in tone: the *Bildungsroman* of a young inhabitant of Glasgow called Duncan Thaw, who wishes to become an artist (in this and many other respects he undoubtedly resembles his author), and who eventually dies and goes to the afterworld. The other half is fantastic and perplexing: in the imaginary cities of Unthank and Provan, a man named Lanark confronts various grotesque transformations, bears witness to Duncan Thaw's life in the 'real' world, enjoys a love tryst, and embarks on journeys through the so-called Intercalendrical Zones. There are suggestions that Lanark and Duncan Thaw are one and the same person;

certainly, the dark city of Unthank – all tenements, shipyards, motorways and waste lots, peopled by folk who grow leathery hides like dragons – resembles a shadowy version of Glasgow, the bad dream of a lifelong native of that industrial metropolis. Towards the end there is an amusing chapter in which Lanark meets his creator, the author. Here the protagonist discovers that his world is made up not of atoms but of print: 'tiny marks marching in neat lines, like armies of insects, across pages and pages and pages of white paper . . . Your survival as a character and mine as an author depend on us seducing a living soul into our printed world and trapping it here long enough for us to steal the imaginative energy which gives us life.'

The author proceeds to lecture his hero on world literature, and the text is suddenly filled with footnotes and marginalia which comment on the whole story and point us towards the author's 'plagiarisms'. We learn that he has quoted from authorities who range from John Milton to James Hadley Chase. Of particular importance to him is the influence of earlier writers of fantasy: Edgar Allan Poe, Lewis Carroll, George MacDonald, Franz Kafka, Jorge Luis Borges and Wyndham Lewis are all acknowledged, as are a couple of the authors and texts we have considered in this *Hundred Best* – William Golding's *Pincher Martin* (*17*) and Flann O'Brien's *The Third Policeman* (*36*); 'modern afterworlds are always infernos, never paradisos, presumably because the modern secular imagination is more capable of debasement than exaltation'. This chapter, and indeed the whole of Gray's odd masterpiece, amounts to a hilarious mock-encyclopedia and a fine tribute to the Great Tradition of the fantastic.

First edition: Edinburgh, Canongate, 1981 (hardcover)
First American edition: New York, Harper & Row, 1981 (paperback)
Most recent edition: London, Grafton (paperback)

78

MICHAEL MOORCOCK

The War Hound and the World's Pain

With upwards of seventy books behind him, some of the earlier ones apparently written in three days flat, Michael Moorcock is now the consummate professional entertainer. These days he produces large ambitious novels such as *Byzantium Endures* (1981), *The Laughter of Carthage* (1984) and *Mother London* (1988). But once in a while he still tosses off a quickie, a seemingly effortless little fantasy which will help pay a few bills (*The Steel Tsar*, 1981, was dedicated: 'To my creditors, who remain a permanent source of inspiration'). I suspect that *The War Hound and the World's Pain* was another such, but nevertheless it makes for a delightful read. It is much superior to the earlier quickies in, say, the 'Dorian Hawkmoon' series. Moorcock has honed his skills over the years, and they now show a fine gleaming edge.

This is the story of Graf Ulrich von Bek, a seventeenth-century German mercenary who falls in love with the lady Sabrina and discovers that both she and he are among the damned. He is trapped in an enchanted castle by Lucifer, is vouchsafed a glimpse of Hell, and is sent on a quest for the Holy Grail. It is the time of the Thirty Years War, that terrible conflict in which no justice was to be found on either side – and when men, women and children died by the hundreds of thousands. Von Bek, though a hardened soldier, has begun to know despair: 'It came to me then that perhaps God had become senile, that He had lost His memory and no longer remembered the purpose of placing Man on Earth. He had become petulant. He had become whimsical. He retained His power over us but could no longer be appealed to.' In these circumstances, Lucifer seems the better master, especially when he offers to restore von Bek's soul in exchange for the legendary Grail – that long-lost vessel which is also known as the Cure for the World's Pain.

The hero sets out on his seemingly hopeless quest, furnished with maps which show the supernatural realms as well as the lands he already knows. He gains a doughty young Cossack as a travelling companion. With the help of the ghostly riders of a Wild Hunt, they cross into the 'Mittelmarch', a country which lies on the borderlands between Earth and Hell, or perhaps between Hope and Desolation. There they find an eccentric sage who lives in a remote happy valley, and he gives them clues as to the whereabouts of the Grail. Meanwhile, there is war in Hell, as various of Lucifer's minions rebel against the Prince of Darkness's 'peace plan'. Von Bek and his friend are beset by terrifying magical foes, but manage to win their way through to the Forest at the Edge of Heaven, where lies the Holy Grail. The nature of the fabled cup turns out to be deceptively simple, and the story ends with an affirmation of humane values.

The War Hound and the World's Pain is a fast-moving and atmospheric tale written in its author's best sour-romantic style. The narrator is characteristically introspective, and is gifted with a sharp eye for the complexity and cruelty of the real world. Although this novel is spun from the stuff of dreams, it does not offer easy reassurances. Moorcock's *The Brothel in Rosenstrasse* (1982) and *The City in the Autumn Stars* (1986) are quasi-sequels which feature later members of the von Bek family at different periods of European history.

First edition: New York, Pocket Books, 1981 (hardcover)
First British edition: London, New English Library, 1982 (hardcover)
Most recent edition: London, NEL (paperback)

79

MICHAEL SHEA

Nifft the Lean

Michael Shea writes fantasies in the Jack Vance vein – his first novel, *A Quest for Simbilis* (1974), was a direct sequel to Vance's *The Eyes of the Overworld*. Yet in his picaresque masterpiece *Nifft the Lean* he transcends the older writer's influence to produce a work which has more in common with the apocalyptic paintings of Hieronymus Bosch than it has with the visions of any other fantasy novelist. Shea's setting may be a conventional 'Dying Earth' of the indeterminate future, just as his hero, the eponymous Nifft, may be an avatar of Vance's Cugel the Clever, but these facts are of relatively small importance. The book is made up of four long stories – the framing device, consisting of an introduction and mock-scholarly prefaces to each of the tales, is tedious and unnecessary. But all this matters little, for the core of the book, its Bosch-like evocations of various netherworlds, is highly original: it reveals a powerful and grotesque imagination at work.

In the first episode, 'Come Then, Mortal – We Will Seek Her Soul', the professional thief, Nifft the Lean, and his proud colleague, Haldar, find themselves surrounded by giant wolves on a lonely plain. They are saved from the beasts' jaws by a goddess-like figure which arises, strewn with maggots and putrescence, from the world of the dead: 'A woman had been born, nude and whole. The earth she lay on was clean, and the air was pure again, though when she moved she still gave off a gust of cold like wind off a glacier. Then she said: "Raise me, mortals, My strength is nearly spent with climbing up to you."' This beautiful apparition, seven years dead, was once crossed in love; her lover failed to honour a suicide pact, and now she demands of the two trickster-thieves that they find the man who thwarted her and bring him to her in the underworld. Fascinated by the challenge, and tempted by possible riches, Nifft and Haldar hurry to fulfil this quest. They kidnap their quarry, a vain, handsome brute now running to fat, and carry him into the afterlife by means of a magic spell. There they eventually deliver him to his cold mistress, but not before they have seen enough to make any hero blench:

> Those waters teemed . . . They glowed, patchily, with a rotten orange light, and in those swirls of light you could see them by the score: the little bug-faced ectoplasms that lifted wet, blind eyes against the gloom, and twiddled their feelers imploringly; and others like tattered snakes of leper's-flesh with single human eyes and lamprey mouths. And there were bigger things too, much bigger . . .
>
> . . . We moved steadily, by what means did not appear, and the water's denizens, as they saw us, all dodged our course. Some were rooted and could not: men whose legs fused and tapered to a stem and whose bodies hung just under the surface with every vein and nerve sprouting out of them, like fan-corals red and grey, and with their brains branching out above like little trees. Crabs with human lips scuttled up and down these nerve-festoons. And everywhere in the water were shoals of armless bald homunculi, fat as sausages, kicking through the darkness.

Much more, and worse, is to come. Nifft harrows a different hell in the even more visionary story called 'The Fishing of the Demon Sea' (in this one the hero literally goes to hell in a hand-cart). Michael Shea's unforgettable sub-worlds owe little to Christianity or to any other traditional mythology. They are amazing creations of the author's fevered imagination.

First edition: New York, DAW Books, 1982 (paperback)
First British edition: London, Granada, 1985 (paperback)

80

MARK HELPRIN

Winter's Tale

This blockbuster by an American author is even longer than Crowley's *Little, Big* or Gray's *Lanark* – nearly 800 pages in the British paperback edition. It has been described by óne reviewer as 'a faerie family saga' and 'the first specifically *capitalist* fantasy' (Mary Gentle, *Interzone*, Spring 1985). It can scarcely avoid being 'capitalist', for it is a book which celebrates New York City, that centre of teeming economic activity (and a scene of breathtaking beauty when it is blanketed by winter snow, as it is throughout much of the novel). But of course this setting is not the real New York; rather, it is an idiosyncratic, fantastical version of that great metropolis, as seen over the span of a hundred years, from around the beginning of the twentieth century to the millennium's end. The characters include gangsters, businessmen, scapegraces, and a lovely white horse that can fly; but the city itself is always at the centre of things, and it is for sure a place which thrives on money: 'Bakers baked their endless rows of cookies; mechanics worked at oily engines that smelled of flint and steel; and bank clerks worked their lines, piecing out and taking in tiny sums through the organizational baleen of their graceful human hands, never knowing that the wealth of great kingdoms was all around them, filtering through the streets of lower Manhattan like a tide in the reeds.'

Peter Lake, the trickster hero, is a foundling, set adrift in a tiny boat by his desperate parents after they have been refused entry to the city of their dreams. This latter-day Moses is eventually caught in the reeds of Manhattan's streets and skyways, and there he grows to maturity – in that 'great and imperfect steel-tressed palace of a hundred million chambers, many-tiered gardens, pools, passages, and ramparts above its rivers.' Like the entire novel, this description epitomizes New York during its classic phase, which is to say the first half of the present century – a futuristic paradise for which many Americans (and citizens of other parts of the globe) now feel a profound nostalgia; needless to say, it is totally unlike the image of New York-as-nightmare depicted in Angela Carter's *The Passion of New Eve* (62). Yet Mark Helprin does not neglect to mention the poverty and squalor of the town he has chosen to glorify: early in the story Peter Lake sees a dying child of the slums, and this vision of hopelessness remains with him throughout the book.

For a while, Peter works for the ruthless gangland boss Pearly Soames, who longs 'to build a golden room in a high place, and post watchmen to watch the clouds. When they turn gold, and the light sprays upon the city, the room will open . . . In the center I will put a simple bed, and there I will repose in warmth and gold . . . for eternity.' But Peter becomes a sworn enemy of Soames and his minions, and spends much of his time on the run from them. At one point, he is cornered and nearly killed, but is saved at the crucial moment by the stray white horse which becomes his boon companion. Together, he and the horse come to the rescue of a dying heiress – Beverly, the consumptive daughter of a newspaper magnate. Love story, *Bildungsroman*, urban picaresque, and apocalyptic fantasy, *Winter's Tale* is a book of many parts. A paean to capitalist values – or a religious parable? Perhaps both. Whatever the case, Helprin's long novel is a haunting piece of North American magic realism.

First edition: New York, Harcourt Brace Jovanovich, 1983 (hardcover)
First British edition: London, Weidenfeld & Nicolson, 1983 (hardcover)
Most recent editions: New York, Pocket Books, and London, Arrow (paperbacks)

81

K. W. JETER
_____

Soul Eater

A young woman lies in a coma following a drug-induced stroke. She is not expected to recover. Unknown to her adoptive sister, who cares for her, and her ex-husband, who visits her at weekends, her brain remains alive. Her warped soul reaches out, malevolently, to take over other people's minds and bodies. The victims are all blood-relations, and among them is her ten-year-old daughter, Dee. The novel's hero, David Braemer, is at first completely ignorant of all this: he is abroad when his ex-wife suffers her brainstorm, and for a full year after she has become comatose he remains unaware of the true horror of the situation. Then one night his apparently loving daughter creeps into the bedroom with a large kitchen knife. He awakes just in time to save his own life, as Dee spits obscenities at him . . .

K. W. Jeter's handling of the characters is strong, and his observation of their surroundings is acute. The book is a spare, taut and intense thriller, set in a contemporary Californian landscape which seems to be littered with wasted lives, failed marriages, estranged parents: 'The current of light and noise on the freeway fell behind the car as he drove. Other fathers, other children, silent or talking as they went from one home to another. The great Sunday evening ritual . . . Braemer saw those other divorced daddies on the street or in the supermarket, could recognize them even in the middle of the week when they didn't have their kids with them, pushing shopping carts stacked with TV dinners and kids' junk food. A fraternal organization that one didn't join but, except for those who had engineered it for themselves, fell into. The freeway sorted it out, sifting the kids back and forth.'

Despite this bleakness (and the horrors which follow) the novel has an optimistic conclusion. Braemer is able to fight the evil and win back his daughter. It transpires that his wife and her good-for-nothing brother have taken part in parapsychological experiments designed to ensure the immortality of their own souls. However, they have been seduced by the 'left-hand-way'. Their former guru comes to Braemer, offering assistance: 'there is more than one kind of permanence that the soul can achieve. The immortality of light and air – and that of the dark earth. One path is long . . . The other path – the *via sinistra* – is quicker, but darkness is at the end of it. One's soul achieves permanence, but that of cold stone, heavy, sinking to the earth's core. Away from the light. And for those who follow that path, the damage begins long before the end is reached. The personality becomes deranged, vicious.'

This fantasy of the supernatural is clearly a metaphor for the way in which certain people try to take over other's lives, and, more specifically, for the way in which selfish parents can damage their children. K.W. Jeter (born 1950) has stated in an interview that he believes children to be the true subject-matter of most modern American horror fiction. Like Stephen King and his many imitators, Jeter deals in the dark side of the Freudian 'family romance'. He does so less sentimentally than King (and for that reason his work is likely to be less popular) but he achieves considerable emotional force. *Soul Eater* was his first novel in this vein, but he has since used similar material in the powerful *Dark Seeker* and *Mantis* (both 1987). Jeter is a writer to watch.

First edition: New York, Tor Books, 1983 (paperback)

82

R. A. MacAVOY

Tea with the Black Dragon

Mrs Martha Macnamara, a middle-aged musician with an interest in Zen Buddhism, travels from New York to San Francisco in order to answer a sudden plea for help from her daughter, Liz. Martha registers at a plush hotel which has been chosen by her daughter, and there she meets a most unusual and compelling man. Mr Mayland Long, as he calls himself, is scholarly, golden-eyed, part-Chinese, apparently ageless – and as strong as an ox, though slimly built. He tells wonderful stories, and hints that he is centuries old. He also claims to have begun life as a Chinese dragon, the Black Dragon, a wise reptilian hoarder of treasure and *objets d'art* who has now given up material things in order to search for Truth.

When Martha has difficulty in tracing her errant daughter, Mayland Long offers to help. Liz works as a systems analyst, but computing is a field her mother knows nothing about. Mr Long says that he is an expert in languages – every type of language, including the arcane speech of computer 'wizards' – and, sure enough, he is able to converse knowledgeably with computer-store owners, university professors and software managers, all of whom give him some leads as to Liz's activities and whereabouts. It soon becomes clear that young Miss Macnamara is caught up in something illegal and highly dangerous, a skein of events which encompasses computer fraud, embezzlement of bank funds, kidnapping and perhaps even murder. Martha and Mr Long are drawn into all this, to their cost, but their intervention ensures that the right side wins in the end.

Tea with the Black Dragon is a charming little novel – part fantasy, part love story, part detective thriller. The plot seems weak, if one judges the book primarily as a mystery story, and the fantasy element is fairly slight, but it is the mixture of these ingredients which gives the story its characteristic flavour. Mayland Long and Martha Macnamara are fresh and engaging characters, far from the stereotyped hero and heroine of most genre fantasies, and their tale is told with a pleasant lightness of touch. The indestructible and omniscient Mayland Long reminds us slightly of Sherlock Holmes, even if his name is more reminiscent of Nayland Smith's – hero of Sax Rohmer's 'Fu Manchu' stories. In fact, Mayland Long is like a benign cross between the intrepid Nayland Smith and the mysterious Dr Fu Manchu himself (that oriental villain of superhuman powers).

This was the first published novel by Roberta MacAvoy, a young writer who has since become a popular and prolific spinner of fantastic tales. Her other books include the *Damiano* trilogy (1983–84), set in Renaissance Italy; *The Book of Kells* (1985), set in medieval Ireland; and *Twisting the Rope* (1986), a sequel to the novel I have been describing here, in which Martha and Mr Long become involved in another Californian caper. *Tea with the Black Dragon* may turn out to be the beginning of a successful mystery series, but in retrospect it can also be seen as one of the first titles in a new surge of American fantasy novels which present us with supernaturally-endowed characters in up-to-date settings – I am thinking of such entertaining examples, in a not dissimilar vein, as Megan Lindholm's *The Wizard of the Pigeons* and Terry Bisson's *Talking Man* (both 1986).

First edition: New York, Bantam, 1983 (paperback)
First British edition: London, Bantam, 1987 (paperback)

83

BRIAN MOORE

Cold Heaven

Like *The Great Victorian Collection* (56), Moore's *Cold Heaven* is a tale of the miraculous in conflict with the mundane. The first three or four chapters are written with a driving intensity which keeps one turning the pages, avidly. Marie Davenport, a lapsed Catholic, is on holiday with her selfish husband, Alex, in the South of France. She is about to leave him for another man, but has not yet plucked up the courage to tell him the news. They paddle out to sea in a tiny boat; Alex plunges into the water for a swim, and Marie watches in horror as he is struck on the head by a passing motorboat. Alex is rushed to the hospital unconscious. Marie accompanies him, fighting a rising sense of dread and guilt. She is instantly aware that she is being 'punished' by supernatural powers – not so much for her adultery, but because she has chosen to ignore a strange event, possibly a divine message, which she experienced on the west coast of America exactly one year before. After long hours of anxious waiting in the foreign hospital, Marie is informed that her husband has died. However, it soon becomes apparent that he will refuse to rest in peace.

It would be wrong of me to recount more of the plot, for this is a novel which depends on its surprises. Like a good Alfred Hitchcock film (*Vertigo*, say), it keeps one in an eerie suspense. The reader enters a world of the uncanny where everyday details have taken on a preternatural significance. *Cold Heaven* is by no means a conventional 'ghost story', nor a mere case study in religious delusion. Nor is it, in any literal sense, a tale of zombies and angels. In the main, it is the story of one modern woman's refusal to be cowed by the inexplicable, the ineffable; it is about a courageous *non serviam*. Although the narrative is told from Marie's point of view, it also evokes sympathy for the husband, Alex – self-obsessed, unimaginative and materialistic as he is. Brian Moore's style is spare but cunningly crafted, and much of the burden of his novel rests on what remains unsaid.

Yet the book has imperfections. The earlier part seems to have been written at white heat, but towards the end the narrative drifts – after the characters have taken up residence in a motel near Carmel, California (very similar to the setting of *The Great Victorian Collection*). There is some unsatisfactory shifting of viewpoint in these later scenes, and the tension slackens. After reading the novel I looked up a newspaper interview with Brian Moore ('The Novelist Who Listens to Women' by Philip Oakes, *Sunday Times*, 4 October 1981) and was impressed by several points. Although he attended a Jesuit school in Ireland, Moore states: 'I never had any faith. I could never forget that my grandfather was a Protestant lawyer who changed his religion to help his business.' Midway through the writing of his first novel, in the 1950s, Moore 'was seriously injured when, out swimming, he was struck on the head by a passing speedboat and taken to hospital with his skull fractured in six places. "Of course it was terrible at the time, but now I believe that a brush with death does wonders for a writer's energy".' The emotional fuel which still flows from this incident obviously adds power to *Cold Heaven*. Moore also remarks in the interview: 'I never know how the story will end. I change my mind along with the characters.' This too is evident from the novel in hand, but it remains a brilliantly written and moving book.

First edition: New York, Farrar, Straus & Giroux, 1983 (hardcover)
First British edition: London, Cape, 1983 (hardcover)
Most recent editions: New York, Fawcett, and London, Granada (paperbacks)

84

TIM POWERS

_____

The Anubis Gates

This book about time travel, ancient Egyptian magic and violent shenanigans in early nineteenth-century London is a romp of a story – sheer entertainment. In the words of a *Times Literary Supplement* reviewer, it is 'a yarn, an adventure novel, convulsed by chases and explosions . . . a supernatural thriller . . . a literary mystery . . .a horror story . . . Plotted with manic fervour, executed with exhilarating dexterity at breakneck speed, *The Anubis Gates* is a virtuoso performance, a display of marvellous fireworks . . .' High praise indeed. Given this gushing response, and the fact that the book won the first Philip K. Dick Memorial Award for the best paperback-original novel of its year, one is tempted to seek out its faults. Tim Powers (born 1952) is an American author, and his attempts to capture the flavour of nineteenth-century British voices often falter – I find it hard to believe that a young Englishwoman of 1810 would use terms like 'I guess' and 'goddamn'. At times this is historical fantasy done in a slapdash Hollywood style, and although Powers takes some pains to evoke period mood, his prose has a regrettable tendency to grow thin as the action comes ever thicker and faster. Still, one is prepared to forgive all this for the sake of the *yarn*.

The hero is an American literary academic named Brendan Doyle. An expert on the Romantic Movement and a particular authority on the work of a minor poet called William Ashbless, Doyle is recruited to the organization of an eccentric businessman who possesses the means of travelling into the past. His task is to act as a sort of tour guide: he accompanies a group of literature-lovers who have paid a million dollars apiece for the privilege of hearing a lecture by Samuel Taylor Coleridge as delivered by the great man himself in a London tavern of the year 1810. The mysterious employer has a secret agenda, however; he seeks immortality, and to this end he wishes to track down 'Dog-Face Joe', a hirsute killer who terrorizes Coleridge's London. It seems that this prodigiously hairy man has the ability to switch bodies – an ability conferred by magic out of Old Egypt. As the unwitting victim of various clashing schemes, the anti-heroic Brendan Doyle soon finds himself trapped in 1810, unable to return to his own time and on the run from a proliferation of gargoyle-like menaces. These include a wizened gypsy sorcerer, a sinister beggar-king on stilts, and, of course, the unspeakable Dog-Face Joe. Sick and impoverished, Doyle is befriended by a young woman who poses as a boy beggar. He also meets Lord Byron. But his best hope is to contact the poet William Ashbless, whose life and work he knows so intimately. Unfortunately, Ashbless fails to appear in London on the day when (according to the historical record) he should arrive, and so Doyle is forced to *become* Ashbless . . .

The plot grows more and more complex, involving a further time-jump back to seventeenth-century London as well as a magical trip to Egypt, before reaching a denouement which ties everything together with a satisfactory, if mad, logic. It all adds up to a most enjoyable narrative, a nicely balanced mix of humour and horror, tricked out with many cunning revelations and a continually engaging grotesquerie. Any reader will remember in particular those scenes set amidst the sewers and underground rivers of the nineteenth-century metropolis: this subterranean kingdom of the beggars is filled with dwarfs, magicians, clowns, whispering madwomen, and such delightful inventions as the Spoonsize Boys – minuscule men who sail the dark Thames in eggshell halves 'equipped with tiny torches, straw masts and folded paper sails.'

First edition: New York, Ace, 1983 (paperback)
First British edition: London, Chatto & Windus, 1985 (hardcover)
Most recent edition: London, Grafton (paperback)

85

MICHAEL BISHOP

Who Made Stevie Crye?

Marketed as a horror novel, Bishop's entertaining book does have its share of terrors, but is in the main a playful metafiction about the real and the fictitious, about the writer and his or her creations. We soon realize that the tricksy title, *Who Made Stevie Crye?*, is a double pun; for this is a tale about who *made* the said Stevie – that is, who brought her into being – as well as about who caused her to weep. The heroine, Mary Stevenson Crye ('her friends called her Stevie') is a young widow who strives to raise two children on her modest income as a freelance author. One day her electric typewriter breaks down and, desperate for a quick repair, she takes it to an unfamiliar maintenance man. She finds this young fellow decidedly creepy, but at least he seems to know his job: 'his pudgy fingers went about their intricate task with unimpeded speed and deftness, a miniature screwdriver flashing spookily from the dim cavern of the machine. "I enjoy fixing typewriters for people who *need* them."'

The next day Stevie's work goes badly, and she is astounded when her machine appears to complete a (misspelled) statement by itself: 'TYPEWRITERS ARE OBNIPOTENT'. Nothing else happens immediately, but in the dark of the night she is awoken by the clatter of keys, and finds that her typewriter has printed out a near-complete story in the style of the regular column which she does for a local newspaper. It is no jolly piece of journalism, however, but a nightmarish ghost story about her husband, who died of cancer at the age of thirty-nine. Clearly some

231

demonic force is now in possession of her typewriter, and is drawing its literary inspiration from her own fears and fantasies, her secret inner life. The next night this is confirmed, horribly, when the machine again produces a story of its own volition – this time about her daughter, who complains of being too hot in bed and unable to move:

> 'Mama, please – you take the covers off me . . . I've already melted, but I'm still hot.'
>
> This refrain enraged Stevie. She grabbed the satin hem of the GE blanket and yanked both it and the sheet beneath it all the way to the foot of the narrow brass bed. Then she began to scream. Her daughter's lower body, from the neck down, consisted of the slimy ruins of her skeletal structure. Her flesh and her internal organs had liquefied, seeping through the permeable membrane of her bottom sheet and into the box springs beneath the half-dissolved mattress, stranding her pitiful rib cage, pelvis and limb bones on the quivering surface . . .
>
> Marella was heedless of her mother's incapacitating hysteria. 'Still hot,' she said. 'Oh, mama, I'm still hot . . .'

Luckily, this gruesome moment turns out to be 'only a fiction' – but for a while the reader is unsure, and as the novel progresses the uncertainty grows as to what is real and what is imaginary. Stevie is visited by the strange young man who repaired her typewriter – is *he* the author of these macabre ravings? – and she is haunted by the skull-like face of his pet capuchin monkey . . .

Who Made Stevie Crye? is a gripping and intelligent tale of the supernatural by an author who is adept at avoiding most of the clichés of the horror genre. Michael Bishop (born 1945) is an ambitious writer, best known for his excellent science fiction novels such as *No Enemy But Time* (1982) and *Ancient of Days* (1985). For him, *Stevie Crye* may be considered a *jeu d'esprit*, but one with a serious sub-text.

First edition: Sauk City, Arkham House, 1984 (hardcover)
First British edition: London, Headline, 1987 (paperback)

86

JAMES P. BLAYLOCK

The Digging Leviathan

'Was there a land at the centre of the earth, a hollow sphere wherein dinosaurs and mythical beasts sported in unimaginable jungles? And could you get there through tide pools off the Los Angeles coast? The clues all indicated that it was so: the legendary polar explorer John Pinion was in Los Angeles, disguised as an ice-cream man and making strange offers to the little boy who had webbed fingers and gills on his neck; old cars and men on bicycles were seen by some to fly over the tree-shaded streets of Glendale at sunset; the dead bodies of what were probably mer-men were found washed up along desolate stretches of the Catalina shore; and William Hastings, maverick science-fiction writer and inmate at a local mental hospital, had found evidence to believe that his doctor was a homicidal madman who was trying to achieve immortality by means of an elixir distilled from dead carp . . .' So says the cover blurb on the British edition of this madcap comedy. What at first appears to be an old-fashioned 'scientific romance', a story of Symmesian holes in the ice-caps and a world at the earth's core à la Edgar Rice Burroughs, turns out to be a gentle but high-spirited fantasy of manners which concerns itself with the extraordinary doings of a collection of zany characters in present-day California.

Apart from Hastings, the lunatic writer who entertains a hundred and one pseudoscientific theories, and Giles Peach, the boy with gills and webbed fingers and an incredible ability to magically 'customize' machines, the characters include an aged, eccentric poet called William Ashbless

(James P. Blaylock shares this character with his friend Tim Powers, author of *The Anubis Gates* (80) – 'Ashbless' was originally their joint pseudonym). We also meet young Jim Hastings, a comparatively level-headed romantic who reads novels about Pellucidar and Fu Manchu, and his likeable uncle, Edward St Ives. All these characters dream of visiting the unknown realm beneath the earth, 'a dark chasm world lit by the flowing lights of gliding submarines and by the occasional lamps of the sewer dwellers, little stars that glinted on distant islands, goblin fires in the black void, miles below the concrete and asphalt lace of surface streets'. One group, led by the explorer Pinion, intends to reach the subterranean world by means of an elaborate mechanical mole, a Digging Leviathan engineered by Giles Peach. The other group, which includes Jim and his uncle and his mad father, means to make the journey by sea – or via the sewers. Neither group succeeds (at any rate, not until the last paragraph of the novel) but their dreams are rich and strange.

The Digging Leviathan is virtually a womanless novel – it certainly has no sexual elements. A delicately-written, poetic farce about a bunch of male obsessives, it is almost a Southern Californian *Tristram Shandy* (the author acknowledges Laurence Sterne in his Postscript to the British edition, agreeing with the earlier writer's sentiment that it is 'more pardonable to trespass against truth, than beauty'). This is not a book which will appeal to all readers, though lovers of hoary scientific romances should respond to many of its densely-packed references. Blaylock's later book, *Homunculus* (1986), gained a Philip K. Dick Memorial Award as best paperback-original novel – but with its rather Americanized nineteenth-century London setting and its resemblance to Powers's *The Anubis Gates* it seems a lesser work than his spendidly original hollow-earth fantasy.

First edition: New York, Ace, 1984 (paperback)
First British edition: Bath, Morrigan Publications, 1988 (hardcover)
Most recent edition: London, Grafton (paperback)

87

ANGELA CARTER

Nights at the Circus

Carter's longest novel to date, and her most highly praised, is built around a central character of gargantuan proportions – an earthy (but airy) heroine as irrepressible as Joyce's Molly Bloom or Michael Moorcock's Mrs Honoria Cornelius. This is the story of a woman with wings, a six-foot-two-inch 'Cockney Venus' named Fevvers, huge of breast and buttock but immensely athletic and the most famous *aerialiste* of her day. She claims to have been hatched rather than born: 'Hatched out of a bloody great egg while Bow Bells rang, as ever is!' Fevvers has a voice like the clatter of dustbin lids, and she likes to shock young men by emitting wind, very audibly, in their presence. She gorges herself on vulgar food: 'hot meat pies with a glutinous ladleful of eel gravy on each; a Fujiyama of mashed potatoes; a swamp of dried peas cooked up again and served swimming in greenish liquor.' Nevertheless Fevvers has just returned from a successful tour of Europe, and has slavish admirers everywhere: they include the artist Toulouse Lautrec and the heir to the British throne, Edward, Prince of Wales. (The story opens in December 1899, in the dying days of the nineteenth century.)

A young American journalist, Jack Walser, comes to London to interview Fevvers, hoping to expose her as a fraud in his series of articles called 'Great Humbugs of the World'. Are her wings made of gutta-percha, or is she a genuine prodigy posing as a showbiz fake? The lady gymnast makes him welcome in her dressing-room and proceeds to tell him the story of her life – with the assistance of her ever-present maid, the mysterious Lizzie, who pulls all manner of documents from her capacious handbag. Fevvers seats the newspaperman among her soiled underwear, attends to him with 'gigantic coquetry', nearly chokes him with her face powder and scent (shades of Marlene Dietrich in *The Blue Angel*), then spellbinds him with her lengthy narrative. As Colin Greenland remarked in his review of this novel in *Interzone*, Walser has come 'to poke the vortex. This is unwise. He gets sucked in. Us too.' Raised by Lizzie in a Whitechapel brothel (with a good supply of books and a sound feminist education), Fevvers first unfurled her wings at the age of fourteen, and learned to fly soon thereafter. Cast out of her first home, she was obliged to take employment with the dreadful Madame Schreck, proprietress of a 'museum of woman monsters'. Here she worked for six months among the female freaks, before being 'bought' by a middle-aged gentleman of perverse tastes – and barely escaping from him with her life. Reunited with her beloved Lizzie, she subsequently became a stage performer, and now is about to embark on a circus tour of Russia and Japan.

The first third of the novel is taken up by Fevvers' reminiscences, told in a style which combines the colloquial and the poetically learned. In the subsequent two-thirds (written at a slightly lower imaginative pitch) the besotted Jack Walser joins the circus and follows his heroine to St Petersburg and, later, to Siberia, where they have sundry adventures on the taiga as the twentieth century dawns. There is a strong suggestion that the mighty Fevvers is a new woman for a new age, the all-embracing, all-conquering, high-soaring symbol of a liberated femininity. Certainly, she humbles Walser and all other men who cross her path – just as effectively as she entrances the reader. Angela Carter has surpassed herself in this rich and flamboyant tale of the never-was. It is a book which is written with great verve, great good humour, great daring and great generosity of spirit.

First edition: London, Chatto & Windus, 1984 (hardcover)
First American edition: New York, Viking, 1985 (hardcover)
Most recent editions: London, Picador, and New York,
Penguin (paperbacks)

88

THOMAS M. DISCH

The Businessman: A Tale of Terror

The opening chapters of this graveyard fantasy are slightly reminiscent of Peter Beagle's *A Fine and Private Place* (*24*), but the story develops in much more horrid ways. Here the supremely talented Thomas Disch (born 1940) invades Stephen King's territory as well as Beagle's – with blackly comical results. The businessman in question is the corpulent Bob Glandier, a denizen of present-day Minneapolis. He is a disgusting specimen of modern American barbarism, totally without redeeming virtues. (Among his many sins is the fact that he relishes the depraved fantasy fiction of John Norman, who argues for 'the essential normalcy of man's need to beat, rape and abuse and, by these means, to dominate the woman he loves'.) Luckily, there are several more sympathetic characters in the novel: Giselle, Glandier's persecuted wife; Joy-Ann Anker, Giselle's mother; Bing Anker, Glandier's homosexual brother-in-law; and, not least, the ghost of the poet John Berryman (who, in actuality, committed suicide in 1972 by jumping from a bridge in Minneapolis).

The story opens as Giselle awakes in her grave. She recalls being murdered by her husband, but she feels little anger. For months her ghostly consciousness hovers just above the rotting remains of her body. 'The worms crawl in,' she thinks dispassionately. 'The worms crawl out. The worms play pinochle on your snout.' She is eventually released from the grave by her dying mother. Joy-Ann Anker has cancer (a nun advises her to smoke marijuana in order to ease the side-effects of chemotherapy), and on visiting Giselle's graveside she sees something which causes her to keel over and die:

> She knelt down to take a closer look at the impossible flower on her daughter's grave, and only when she was on her knees did she see that it wasn't a flower at all that blossomed from the plant's thick stem but a small pink hand. It grasped Joy-Ann's finger and tugged at it, as a child might, struggling to keep its balance as it took its first faltering steps.
>
> Just as Joy-Ann died, Giselle's voice shrilled delightedly in her ears: *Mummy, I'm free! Oh, thank you so much.*

However, Giselle is not quite as free as she had hoped. She is still tied to the earthly plane, and is doomed to haunt her monstrous husband. Meanwhile, her mother has a fine old time in the anteroom of the afterlife, where she enjoys all modern conveniences while watching reruns of her own past existence on Home Box Office (she also makes the acquaintance of a couple of poets, including the suicidal but penitent John Berryman).

Giselle's haunting of Bob Glandier is a rum affair, and its consequences are grotesque in the extreme. Glandier impregnates the ghostly Giselle (involuntarily) and she gives birth to a 'halfling' which proceeds to wreak murderous havoc among both the living and the dead. The halfling comes close to killing the inoffensive Bing Anker, Giselle's brother, who has returned home to attend their mother's funeral; but in the end both Glandier and his vile offspring are thwarted by the combined forces of the good characters. The fat businessman dies and is consigned to his own peculiar hell, while Bing lives on; and Giselle, Joy-Ann and John Berryman all ascend to the higher planes of heaven, each in his or her own fashion. Thus Disch's novel emerges as an irreligious morality tale – stylishly written, occasionally heartless, and rather terrifying in its comic vision of the emptiness of life.

First edition: New York, Harper & Row, 1984 (hardcover)
First British edition: London, Cape, 1984 (hardcover)
Most recent edition: London, Grafton (paperback)

89

ROBERT HOLDSTOCK

Mythago Wood

This memorable 'Matter-of-Britain' fantasy is the best book so far by the English writer Robert Holdstock (born 1948), previously known for his science fiction novels such as *Eye Among the Blind* (1976) and *Where Time Winds Blow* (1982). The setting is Ryhope Wood, Herefordshire: 'Three square miles of original, post-Ice Age forestland. Untouched, uninvaded for thousands of years.' The time is the late 1940s, and the narrator is a young man named Steven Huxley. He returns from war service abroad to find his family home, Oak Lodge, in a run-down state. During Steven's absence his father had died, raving of 'oak vortices' and 'mythago zones', and now his elder brother, Christian, seems to have developed the same inexplicable obsessions. The latter disappears into the woodland for days or weeks at a time, to return 'scratched and scarred from neck to ankle, filthy, and malodorous to an extreme . . . as if he had spent the days away buried in compost.' Meanwhile Steven reads his father's diaries, and learns the true nature of the 'research' which wrecked the old man's life and which is now apparently ruining his eldest son's.

It seems that this scrap of unspoiled forest has magical properties. Time and space are distorted in the heartwoods; the area is much greater in extent than it appears to be, and it is full of mysterious forces which are capable of drawing images (myth-images or 'mythagoes') from the depths of the human mind. These images from the collective unconscious take on fleshly form, and can be highly dangerous – and alluring. Many of them are thousands of years old, and they carry a rich freight of historical associations. As Christian Huxley explains to his brother: 'The form of the idealized myth, the hero figure, alters with cultural changes, assuming the identity and technology of the time. When one culture invades another – according to father's theory – the heroes are made manifest . . .' Thus there is a 'Robin Hood' mythago and a 'King Arthur' mythago, and another which dates from the Iron Age, and – behind them all – a terrifying primal mythago from the Stone Age, known as the Urscumug.

Christian Huxley has fallen in love with one particularly beautiful creature of the woods, Guiwenneth: 'She was my father's mythago, a girl from Roman times, a manifestation of the Earth Goddess, the young warrior princess who, through her own suffering, can unite the tribes.' She has been killed by an arrow from another mythago (it is when Steven discovers Guiwenneth's corpse that he is first convinced of the reality of these preternatural beings), but Christian continues to explore the endless, labyrinthine wildwood in the hope that she has been 'reborn'. In time, Steven follows him, and the two have a hair-raising encounter with the man-beast which their father named the Urscumug. Many wonderful and uncanny events occur thereafter, and the atmosphere of the greenwood, both romantic and brutal, is beautifully evoked.

Mythago Wood has been described by Alan Garner as 'a new expression of the British genius for true fantasy'. The raw subject-matter is scarcely novel – 'Celtic' fantasies are two-a-penny these days – but the way in which it has been deployed here is fresh and ingenious. Certainly Holdstock uses his traditional material to create a whole new range of pleasurable *frissons*. The book was a deserving winner of the World Fantasy Award, and a sequel, to be called *Lavondyss*, has been promised for the near future.

First edition: London, Gollancz, 1984 (hardcover)
First American edition: New York, Arbor House, 1985 (hardcover)
Most recent editions: London, Grafton, and New York, Berkley (paperbacks)

90

CHRISTOPHER PRIEST

The Glamour

The dictionary tells us that an archaic meaning of the word 'glamour' is 'magic spell' or 'enchantment', and it is in this sense that Christopher Priest uses the term. As it happens, *The Glamour* is also a wonderfully intriguing title for a book – one asks oneself: what can it be about? It proves to be an understated novel about an Invisible Man, although in this case the invisibility is of a very different sort to the chemically induced 'transparency' which drove H.G. Wells's Dr Griffin to madness. Here the phenomenon is much more akin to the non-visibility of those characters who step outside the clockwork of daily life in Fritz Leiber's *The Sinful Ones*. But Priest's novel comes a quarter of a century after Leiber's, and in fact the resemblance between the two stories is slight. (Oddly enough, invisibility is a fantastic device which has come into fashion once more – other recent treatments of it in fiction include Thomas Berger's *Being Invisible* and H.F. Saint's *Memoirs of an Invisible Man*, both published in 1987.)

Throughout its first half the novel scarcely seems to be a fantasy at all, and more of a straightforward love story tinged by mystery. Richard Grey, a television-news cameraman, is recovering from injuries sustained in a terrorist bomb blast. He suffers from partial amnesia, and has forgotten the details of several weeks of his life prior to the explosion. A young woman, Susan Kewley, comes to visit him in the sanatorium. Richard has no recollection of her, though she claims to be a former girlfriend. He rapidly becomes obsessed with her, and as he does so it seems that his memories are beginning to return. We enter a long flashback, in which Richard recounts his lost experiences in the weeks leading up to the blast. He describes a trip to the south of France, during which he first meets Susan and falls in love with her. The idyll is short-lived. He goes on to tell of their curious 'haunting' by Susan's former boyfriend, Niall. The latter is with them in France, an unseen presence who gradually wedges himself between Richard and Susan, forcing them apart.

This Niall is perhaps the leading character of the novel, though he is invisible throughout. There is even a suggestion at the end that the entire narrative (which shifts viewpoint continually) is somehow filtered through his consciousness. Richard's account of the French holiday turns out to be a retrospective illusion. According to Susan's version of events, the couple first met in London, where she gradually introduced Richard to the frightening underworld of 'the glams' – those folk like herself (intermittently) and Niall (at all times) who have the Glamour, which is to say the ability to cloud normal people's minds and render themselves invisible. There are some extraordinary scenes in the latter part of the book – in particular, a rape scene in which the invisible Niall violates Susan while she is in the act of making love to Richard; and a hair-raising episode in which Susan attempts to prove her talent for invisibility by entering a strange house at night and exposing herself to the unseeing eyes of the men within.

It is a compelling narrative, very subtly constructed and full of surprises. Christopher Priest (born 1943) has a rather flat prose style which is more than compensated for by a marvellous ability to deliver the unexpected. *The Glamour* is intentionally deceptive and mystifying, and the openness of the ending will leave some readers dissatisfied. But I find it to be a moving and thought-provoking novel – one of the strangest love-triangle stories ever penned.

First edition: London, Cape, 1984 (hardcover)
First American edition: New York, Doubleday, 1985 (hardcover)
Most recent edition: London, Abacus (paperback; revised version)

91

JOHN UPDIKE

The Witches of Eastwick

I hesitated over the inclusion of this title, on the grounds that John Updike (born 1932) needs no praise from me. Sharp delineator of suburban character and master of a poetic prose style, he has long been one of America's most lauded novelists. But his first full-length venture into fantasy is too good a book to miss; like Amis's *The Green Man* (42), to which it bears a faint resemblance, it is both a fine novel and an excellent genre piece. Its minutely observed social realism only serves to enhance the power of its supernatural content.

It is the time of Nixon and Vietnam. The place is Eastwick, Rhode Island, a seaside town of old New England, where in these days 'windowless little plants with names like Dataprobe and Computech manufactured mysteries, components so fine the workers wore plastic caps to keep dandruff from falling into the tiny electro-mechanical works.' But such faceless technology belongs to the discredited world of men. The novel's central characters, Alexandra, Jane and Sukie, are attractive divorcées in their thirties. Each feels that getting rid of her husband has been an immense liberation. They have discovered new powers in themselves, have become drawn to each other, and have formed a 'coven'. They are witches, of a very matter-of-fact sort, capable of summoning thunderstorms, breaking an old lady's imitation-pearl necklace from a distance, placing dust and feathers in the mouth of a shrewish gossip. Their magic is minor-league stuff, often malicious but scarcely downright evil. They relish the internecine wars of small-town politics and social life, and are able to turn anything and anyone to their advantage. Energetic and likeable women, they use their bodies, their intelligence, their wit, their creative powers; and in their hands even food seems a magical weapon: 'Jane Smart loved devilled eggs, chalky and sharp with paprika and a pinch of dry mustard, garnished with chopped chives or an anchovy laid across each stuffed white like the tongue of a toad.'

There arrives from New York a brash, bearish man named Darryl Van Horne. An apparently rich inventor and art collector, he renovates a large old house near Eastwick, and soon becomes an object of local fascination – even to the trio of witches, so accustomed to ruling their own roost. Van Horne is noisy, opinionated, coarse and detestable, yet all three are drawn to him, inexorably. He draws them out, and before long the three witches are sharing the delights of his vast teak bathroom. It becomes a throughly modern, 'liberated' Sabbat: 'On the black velour mattress Van Horne had provided, the three women played with him together, using the parts of his body as a vocabulary with which to speak to one another; he showed supernatural control, and when he did come his semen, all agreed later, was marvellously cold.' (Earlier on, the author quoted the testament of a sixteenth-century witch who described the Devil as 'cauld lyke yce'.)

The Witches of Eastwick is a realistic, funny and ultimately tragic story of devil-worship. The sexual detail is copious and explicit, and the book has been accused by some readers of being misogynistic, but the high quality of the writing and the ways in which the author gets under the skin of each of his characters (especially the women) make this much more than a pornographic or sexist fantasy. The book has been successfully filmed by the Australian director George Miller: I have yet to see the movie, but it is hard to imagine a cinematic equivalent of Updike's 'transports of spectacular prose' (in the words of a *Time Magazine* reviewer). The author's prose is spectacular and transporting indeed – to such an extent that this becomes one of those works which renew my faith in the novel as a story-telling form which can never be displaced by newer media, however awe-inspiring their special effects.

First edition: New York, Knopf, 1984 (hardcover)
First British edition: London, Deutsch, 1984 (hardcover)
Most recent editions: New York, Fawcett, and
Harmondsworth, Penguin (paperbacks)

92

PETER ACKROYD

Hawksmoor

It won great praise from literary critics on its first publication in Britain, and deservedly so. Peter Ackroyd (born 1949) is a talented pasticheur, and his adoption of an early eighteenth-century voice in much of the novel works brilliantly. That voice belongs to an English architect, an imaginary assistant of Sir Christopher Wren's, called Nicholas Dyer. (The character may be fictional, but it is evident from Ackroyd's choice of title that he is based on the real-life Nicholas Hawksmoor, architect of several London churches.) Dyer tells his story in the language, punctuation and spelling of his own day – perhaps more seventeenth-century than eighteenth, since he is old enough to remember the Great Plague of 1665. It is a racy, humorous style, simultaneously coarse and learned, the style of a man who is both highly intelligent and supremely cynical. Nicholas Dyer was orphaned during the plague, and the experience has left a permanent mark on his psyche; convinced of humanity's inevitable 'corrupcion', he has long since embraced the black arts and become a worshipper of Satan. Each of his churches is secretly dedicated to evil, and each demands a human sacrifice in order to 'consecrate' it. As the foundations of his holy buildings are laid, Dyer arranges a series of apparently fortuitous deaths . . .

Interwoven with this gruesome narrative are chapters which deal with parallel events in present-day London. A number of unfortunates, most of them young boys, are found strangled in the grounds of old churches; but apart from the obvious injuries there are no signs of an assailant. The policeman who investigates the puzzling sequence of murders, one Inspector Hawksmoor of New Scotland Yard, begins to suspect that they can be explained only in supernatural terms. He becomes unhealthily obsessed with the case, and is ordered to take a rest; but nevertheless he learns the identity of the 300-year-old murderer, his *Doppelgänger*. The atmosphere of these contemporary chapters is dismal, chilling, continually haunted by an unspeakable past. This London of the 1980s cannot shake off the contagion of bygone suffering, for the very ground beneath its bricks and tarmac is crammed with the bones of the dead. The effect is frightening in the extreme, making this one of the most blood-curdling ghost stories ever written.

At one point, the despicable Dyer expresses the theme of the novel with his customary fluency: 'We live off the Past: it is in our Words and our Syllables. It is reverberant in our Streets and Courts, so that we can scarce walk across the Stones without being reminded of those who walked there before us; the Ages before our own are like an Eclipse which blots out the Clocks and Watches of our present Artificers and, in that Darkness, the Generations jostle one another. It is the dark of Time from which we come and to which we will return.' There are opposing voices in the novel: Sir Christopher Wren plays an important part in Dyer's story, and his is the voice of sweet reason (even if he is depicted by the narrator as a complacent Pangloss). In one of the most entertaining scenes, we witness a meeting of the Royal Society and are treated to a lecture by Wren in which he claims that 'this is a learned and inquisitive Age . . . an Age of Industry: it will be as a Beacon for the Generations to come, who will examine our Works and say, It was then that the World began anew.' But in spite of this affirmation it is the evil Dyer who dominates the novel: he is an astounding creation, a monster worthy of a place beside Mr Hyde, Dr Moreau and Count Dracula in the pantheon of horror fiction.

First edition: London, Hamish Hamilton, 1985 (hardcover)
First American edition: New York, Harper & Row, 1986 (hardcover)
Most recent editions: London, Abacus, and New York, Harper (paperbacks)

93

LISA GOLDSTEIN

The Dream Years

This highly unusual timeslip romance is the first adult novel by a young writer who won an American Book Award for her children's fantasy *The Red Magician* (1982). I find that the principal subject-matter – the antics of the members of the surrealist movement in Paris during the 1920s – makes a welcome change from the more predictable concerns of most contemporary fantasies. The author says in her prefatory note: 'André Breton, Louis Aragon, Jacques Rigaut, Antonin Artaud, Yves Tanguy, and Paul Eluard were real people. All the other characters are probably fictional.' The hero, Robert St Onge, is a young acolyte of André Breton and those other poets and artists who believe in putting their lives in the service of the unconscious. A would-be novelist, Robert leads the bohemian life of Paris, helping the surrealists arrange their ill-attended readings and exhibitions. In the first chapter, a fortune-teller says to him: 'You will travel farther than anyone . . . you will go on a journey of surpassing strangeness.' But it is no literal journey to Africa or the Moon which she foresees.

Robert encounters a young woman, Solange, and as he follows her through the streets of Paris he passes into another world. He finds himself among rioting students and armoured police, with the scent of revolution in the air: these are *les évènements* of 1968. Somehow Robert has travelled over forty years into the future. Thoroughly bewildered, he soon slips back to his own time; but in the following days he keeps glimpsing Solange, and pursues her obsessively. Meanwhile, under the pressure of these strange happenings and his own doubts about the surrealist movement, Robert breaks with the domineering André Breton and begins serious work on his long-delayed novel. '"A novel?" André laughed. "The novel's dead – don't waste your time. The novel takes a small – oh, infinitely small – cut-and-dried section of so-called reality and calls it art. Your life is art. Don't waste it trying to write a novel."' As he comes to know the mysterious girl better, Robert makes more frequent visits to her frightening but heady future world. Solange, who is a fervent partisan in the 1968 events, attempts to explain to him: 'Time is in flux – we can't always control what's happening . . . When the conditions are right, you can walk through time . . . We realized we needed help, and we thought we could get that help from the past. And we thought that the surrealists, since they were the closest to us in spirit, could help us the most.'

She has studied the history of surrealism, and has seen the parallels between its endeavour to remake the world imaginatively and the similar attemps of her student-revolutionary comrades. Although he finds himself falling in love with her, Robert is irked by Solange's demand that he lend his approval to her revolution: 'Why couldn't you have left me alone, left me to write my novel in peace? You can't ask me to fight a revolution I don't believe in.' Nevertheless he goes with her again into the future – not only to 1968, but even further ahead, to the twenty-first century and another time of upheaval in Paris, when the ideals of both 1924 and 1968 seem to be coming to fruition at last. André Breton and some of the other surrealists accompany them on this ultimate trip, each reacting in his own way to the extraordinary sights that are revealed. Good-humoured and engagingly written, *The Dream Years* is a playful work which deals with serious ideas.

First edition: New York, Bantam, 1985 (hardcover)
First British edition: London, Allen & Unwin, 1986 (papcrback)
Most recent editions: New York, Bantam, and London, Unwin (papcrbacks)

94

GUY GAVRIEL KAY

The Fionavar Tapestry

This is another three-volume heroic fantasy, School of J. R. R. Tolkien. Indeed Guy Gavriel Kay (born 1954, in Canada) has a reputation as a 'Tolkien scholar', having assisted Christopher Tolkien in the task of editing his father's posthumous book *The Silmarillion*. No doubt this gives authority to Kay's statement that 'to be successful in fantasy, you have to take the measure of Tolkien – work with his strengths and away from his weaknesses.' The three books of *The Fionavar Tapestry* are: *The Summer Tree* (1985), *The Wandering Fire* (1986) and *The Darkest Road* (1987).

In the first of these, five Toronto University students – Jennifer, Kimberly, Kevin, Dave and Paul – are whisked away to a faery land by a magician known as Loren Silvercloak. Fionavar is the prime world of all the alternative worlds created by the 'Weaver'. If Fionavar should fall to the evil power of Rakoth Maugrim the Unraveller then all the other worlds will fall too. Inevitably, our five protagonists are recruited to the mighty cause of saving the universe. So far, so familiar – but Kay's lengthy narrative is developed with an ingenuity, and a loving care, which has rarely been matched by anyone since the Master himself. In *The Wandering Fire* one of the five, Jennifer, has a baby by the dark god, Rakoth Maugrim (who raped her at the end of the first volume): perhaps the child's nature will be equally balanced between good and evil. Another of the five, Kimberly, recruits the help of none other than the resurrected King Arthur (and Jennifer is revealed to be a reincarnated Guinevere). Yet another of the group, Paul (who has become 'Lord of the Summer Tree'), sails with Loren Silvercloak and King Arthur to defeat a renegade Mage who has caused drought (and worse) to waste the land. Below the castle they find Sir Lancelot in his long sleep, and Arthur awakes him.

The mythological elements come thick and fast, as all five of the young folk from our world take on sundry mythical roles. The introduction of Arthurian characters could have unbalanced the story at this point, and would certainly have done so in a one-volume novel. However, Kay's tale is sufficiently dense and complex to stand the shock. In the third volume, *The Darkest Road*, everyone limbers up for the final battle. Jennifer's son, now miraculously grown, suffers confusion in his need to choose between darkness and light. In the end, he chooses well, and is instrumental in destroying his terrible father, Rakoth. Following which, Jennifer (Guinevere) remains with King Arthur and Sir Lancelot in Fionavar, and only two of her comrades elect to return to dull Toronto.

The trilogy is smoothly written, in a style which is not too ostentatiously poetic. Kay's use of ordinary young people from our familiar world enables him to give his central characters convincing 'modern' personalities, but the more exotic denizens of Fionavar are also well depicted. The invented world is clearly conceived and well described. The wealth of disparate mythological elements is justified by the fact that this is supposed to be the prime world of the Weaver (of which our own Earth is but one pale shadow) – and the closely woven texture of myths and themes is pointed up by the recurrent imagery of the Weaver and the Tapestry. There are echoes of Tolkien, Alan Garner and Joy Chant, but Guy Gavriel Kay has gleefully ransacked so many other, more traditional, sources that spotting the derivations becomes a pointless game. Metaphysics, magic and morality work together to provide a satisfactory and coherent framework and justification for this enjoyable story.

First British editions: London, Allen & Unwin, 1985–87 (hardcovers)
First American editions: New York, Arbor House, 1985–87 (hardcovers)
Most recent editions: London, Unwin Hyman, and New York, Ace (paperbacks)

95

IAIN BANKS

The Bridge

A man crashes his car on the Forth road bridge in Scotland. As he lies in a deep coma he struggles to remake his life from within. He progresses through a series of bizarre fantasies (most of them involving a vast bridge which seems to link nowhere to nowhere) until at last he reaches a new understanding of himself, and awakes. In bald outline, Iain Banks's novel sounds slightly banal, but of course this outline does not allow for the richness and energy of the author's imagination. Like Alasdair Gray's *Lanark*, this is very much a Scottish book, part of a 1980s renaissance of imaginative literature from Scotland which owes nothing to the J.M. Barrie tradition of sentimental fantasy – although it probably owes a good deal to an older, darker tradition of Presbyterian nightmares, of which James Hogg's *Confessions of a Justified Sinner* is a notable nineteenth-century example.

John Orr (as he is known in this dreamworld) awakes with no memory of his past, and finds himself among the endless steel girders of an enormous bridge – a Forth railway bridge which has expanded to encompass the world. Steam trains thunder past on the lower levels. Above them are tier upon tier of sleeping quarters, workshops, offices, restaurants, all linked together by elevators and tramlines. At first Orr has a privileged place in the hierarchical society of the bridge: he is under the care of one Dr Joyce, who orders him to write down all his dreams. Dreams within dreams: Orr fantasizes about meeting his *Doppelgänger* in a high mountain pass at night; about ships locked in hopeless battle; about a man in rags who flails at the sea with a set of rusty iron chains; about a shore full of beautiful women who tantalize him with their erotic displays . . . But he fails to remember how he came to arrive on the bridge. Eventually he rebels against the doctor's regime, and is punished with demotion to the lowest level of the bridge's society. He is a non-person, and his only course is to become a stowaway on a long-distance train – to travel in hope of finding an end to the geometrical tyranny of the bridge.

Interweaved with all this are other narratives, the most memorable of which concerns a sword-swinging barbarian who recounts his rough adventures in broad Scots. At one point, while searching the underworld for a means to cross the River Lethe, this foul-mouthed Glaswegian Conan has a run-in with Sisyphus:

> Stil ded thirsty an nota sign of a pub or enytin, just aw these rocks an this river flowin slowly past. Ah wandered along the bank fur a bit an found this punter shovin a big round boulder up this hill. Lookt like he did this a lot, judjin from the groov hed worn in the hillside. 'Haw Jimmy,' ah sez, 'ahm lookin for this ferry; whare dae ye catch the steamer aboot here? There a pier here-aboots, aye?' Basturt didnae even turn roond. Rold this huge fukin chuckie right tae the tap aw the hill. But then the rok cums rollin aw the way bak down agen, and the ignorant buggir chases aftir it an starts rollin it back up the hill agen. 'Hi you,' ah sez (didnae hav eny effect). 'Hi, hied-the-baw; whare's the fukin pier fur the steamer?' Ah slapt the basturd over the arse wi the flat ov ma sord an went in frunt of the big stane he was rollin up the hil an lent agenst it to stop him.
>
> Just ma fukin luk; the bampot didnae evin speek proppir; sum forin lingo. Aw shite, ah wiz thinkin . . .

The episodes concerning the barbarian and his highly educated familiar are hilariously funny, and they add much

to the riotous blend of fantasy which comprises *The Bridge*.
It is a pleasing novel.

First edition: London, Macmillan, 1986 (hardcover)
Most recent edition: London, Pan (paperback)

96

RAMSEY CAMPBELL

The Hungry Moon

'Lunacy, lycanthropy, and mooncalves, inhuman things that grew in the womb, were all blamed on the moon. Hecate, goddess of the witches, had originally been a moon goddess with three faces, who had been accompanied by a pack of infernal dogs . . .' And even today the moon may breed white, slug-like monstrosities which will bring panic to an entire community. *The Hungry Moon*, a lunar tale of terror if ever there was one, is a recent novel by 'Britain's answer to Stephen King', John Ramsey Campbell (born 1946). The author's first novel, *The Doll Who Ate His Mother* (1976), was a grisly tale of psychological horror, and since then Campbell has published a string of excellent shockers. As a matter of fact, he was far from being a new writer in the mid-1970s, having published his first book (a collection of Lovecraftian tales) in 1964 – at the astonishingly early age of eighteen. H.P. Lovecraft was Campbell's first love, and the influence of the American writer is still remotely discernible in this grotesque story of an ancient and malevolent deity which returns to haunt a present-day Derbyshire village.

It is a long novel, with a large (and sometimes confusing) cast of characters. Chief among them is Diana Kramer, a young American schoolteacher who comes to work in the small town of Moonwell. The place takes its name from a mysterious pot-hole which lies in a stony bowl on the moors just above the village: 'Presumably someone had once thought it looked wide or deep enough to lose the moon in . . . even at high noon in summer you couldn't

258

see the bottom; walls that looked smooth and slippery as tallow plunged straight into darkness . . .' The local children come here once a year to dress the cave's opening with flowers, an apparently harmless custom which dates back to pagan times. However, another American visitor, a religious fanatic named Godwin Mann, fiercely denounces 'these druidic rites' and sets up camp on the moor in an attempt to put a stop to the age-old ceremony. He soon succeeds in converting most of the villages to his unforgiving brand of fundamentalist Christianity (Ramsey Campbell is very good at portraying the tyranny of the petty-minded and the obsessive). A few brave people, including Diana Kramer and her new boyfriend, a newspaperman from Manchester, remain sceptical. And then the foolish preacher decides to demonstrate the power of God's protection by descending into the pot-hole . . .

The supernatural horror which begins to unfold after Godwin Mann's re-emergence from the inky cave is meticulously described in a long, slow, nerve-racking build-up which fills the latter two-thirds of the novel. Some of the ghastly events might seem ludicrous if described out of context, but they are capable of scaring the reader who willingly submits to Campbell's nightmare logic and edgy prose style. I have never read a story in which simple *darkness*, that ancient bugaboo, plays such a large and effective part. The lunar entity which arises from the moorland pit robs Moonwell of its sunlight and its electrical power, and prevents anyone from escaping the environs of the town. It also poses a threat to a nearby nuclear missile base. Long after I have forgotten the characters and plot-details of this novel, I shall remember the scenes in which terrified people stumble through a world almost entirely bereft of light. The book could well have been entitled *Darkness at Noon*.

First edition: New York, Macmillan, 1986 (hardcover)
First British edition: London, Century Hutchinson, 1987 (hardcover)
Most recent editions: New York, Tor, and London, Arrow (paperbacks)

97

KEN GRIMWOOD

Replay

This is a story based on one of the most seductive of all daydream fantasies – the dream of reliving one's adult life, with the full knowledge of where one went wrong the first time around. The opening line of the novel is a splendid hook: 'Jeff Winston was on the phone with his wife when he died.' Forty-three-year-old Jeffrey Winston dies of an apparent heart attack in the year 1988. He is instantly 'reborn' in 1963, in the the body of his eighteen-year-old self. Young, physically fit and carefree, he retains all his memories – of an unhappy marriage, a mediocre career as a radio journalist, and twenty-five years of fading hopes. Once he has recovered from his initial disorientation, and learned to accept his strange good fortune, he will live this replay of his life to the full. He will earn a vast fortune, win the love of beautiful women, travel the world, perhaps even change the course of history by preventing Lee Harvey Oswald from assassinating President John F. Kennedy . . .

Jeff succeeds in reaching all these goals, though the results are not quite as he expected. He places a bet on the Kentucky Derby (having fortuitously recalled the winning horse's name), then uses his winnings as a much larger stake in another race. Eventually he has hundreds of thousands of dollars with which to play the stock market. Setting up his own company, 'Future, Inc.', he invests in IBM, Xerox, Polaroid, and all those high-tech corporations which he knows will do well in the years to come. Thus he rapidly becomes a multi-millionaire. Meanwhile he has abandoned his college sweetheart and taken up with a good-time girl from Las Vegas. Wealth and sexual gratification are not enough to satisfy him, however, and so he attempts to save Kennedy from the killer's bullet, in the hope that the young President will lead the nation 'towards who knew what – continued prosperity, racial harmony, an early disengagement from Vietnam?' But this effort to forestall Lee Harvey Oswald proves to be Jeff's first major disappointment, and makes him realize that his power to change the world is severely limited.

Wearying of his hedonistic lifestyle, Jeff opts for respectability, marriage and fatherhood. The years pass, until he finds himself at the age of forty-three again, a much happier man than in his first round of life but still essentially unfulfilled. As before, he dies, suddenly and shockingly, despite all the medical precautions that money can buy. And, as before, he reawakens in 1963, a teenage college student once more. He proceeds to build a whole new life, in the terrible knowledge that when the year 1988 comes round for the third time he will certainly be flung back to the beginning of things again. He has become caught in a time-loop, apparently condemned to an endless replay of the same twenty-five-year period. So it goes, until the day, halfway through his third replay, when he happens to see a film called *Starsea* – which is directed by Steven Spielberg, and written by one Pamela Phillips. History has been changed after all, if in a minor way: it would seem that the mysterious Ms Phillips is also trapped in an all-too-familiar cycle of events. She is a fellow 'replayer', and from this point on Jeff is not alone in his predicament.

The plot of Ken Grimwood's novel becomes ever more complex, and remains surprising right up to the end. The book is written in a serviceable style, occasionally marred by conventional political pieties and a little too much sex 'n' sentimentality of the American 'best-seller' kind. But it is a compulsive read, clever and moving and original. Despite a superficial similarity to such recent hit movies as *Back to the Future* and *Peggy Sue Got Married*, no one has produced a time fantasy quite like this one before.

First edition: New York, Arbor House, 1986 (hardcover)
First British edition: London, Grafton, 1987 (hardcover)
Most recent editions: New York, Berkley, and London,
Grafton (paperbacks)

98

GEOFF RYMAN

_____

The Unconquered Country:
A Life History

Although his powerful fantasy novel *The Warrior Who Carried Life* (1985) reached book form first, Ryman really made his name with the magazine version of his novella *The Unconquered Country*. (It originally appeared in *Interzone*, a British quarterly of sf and fantasy, in 1984.) It was voted the most popular story of its year by the magazine's readers, and subsequently won a World Fantasy Award. As a book, it runs to not much more than a hundred pages, but it is undoubtedly a major work in every other respect. The narrative deals very movingly with the tragedy of Cambodia (Kampuchea) in the 1970s – as seen through a distorting lens of the imagination which makes the pain and the pathos of the real events seem more bearable, without diminishing them.

Cambodia is not actually mentioned in the body of the text, although the author makes clear in an afterword that this is certainly the 'unconquered country' he has in mind. The story describes the life of a young woman who is known simply as Third Child. She is a refugee in a city called Saprang Song, and she sells her blood and other parts of her body in order to make a living. She rents out her womb in order to grow machinery, household appliances, and, occasionally, weapons: 'The weapons would come gushing suddenly out of her with much loss of blood, usually in the middle of the night: an avalanche of glossy, freckled, dark brown guppies with black, soft eyes and bright rodent smiles full of teeth. No matter how ill or exhausted Third felt, she would shovel them, immediately, into buckets and tie down the lids. If she didn't do that, immediately, if she fell asleep, the guppies would eat her.' This startling imagery, which crystallizes so much of Third World economic reality, is typical of all that is to follow in the novella.

We hear about the Neighbours, a nation which has 'coveted the lands of Third's people for generations', and we hear of the Big People who give terrible weapons to the Neighbours. Third Child's early years were spent in a country village, in a house which lived and breathed: 'The houses of the people were alive. They lived for generations, with wattles and wrinkles and patches of whisker, like ancient grannies . . . They knew their families and cared for them.' But winged monsters known as sharks attacked from the air, and (with the help of the Neighbours) they drove the surviving Unconquered People from their villages and into the festering, overcrowded city. Here folk live in the dead husks of houses, piled one atop the other, and here Third must learn to sell pieces of herself in order barely to survive. However, her new life has its joyful moments: she is courted by a man called Crow, and gradually comes to love him. But their brief happiness is soon broken by the resumption of war.

The rebels win their battles – and then order everyone to leave the city. The story builds to a devastating climax when Third is trapped on a bridge along with thousands of other refugees: 'The faces of the People were the faces of the Dead – bloated and unmoving and lopsided, with open mouths . . . You are all Dead, she thought, we are all crossing over. The thought made her feel peaceful and at home; all of her friends were Dead. In the city behind, brown clouds of smoke were rising up.' And Third's final apotheosis, when it comes, is intensely moving. For all its grim subject-matter, *The Unconquered Country* is a brave and magical fable – hard-edged, lyrical and curiously uplifting.

First edition: London, Allen & Unwin, 1986 (hardcover)
First American edition: New York, Bantam, 1987 (paperback)
Most recent edition: London, Unwin (paperback)

99

J. G. BALLARD

The Day of Creation

Doris Lessing has described this book as a 'phantasmago-ria', and Angela Carter has called it a 'metaphysical adventure story'. *The Day of Creation* may not fit everyone's definition of fantasy, but, however one labels it, it is far from being a realistic novel. J. G. Ballard's preceding book, the best-selling *Empire of the Sun* (1984), was a transmutation of his own childhood experiences during World War II, and could be described as a work of 'heightened' realism. But here he is once more exploring the mindscape of Ballard-land, a fabulous and disquieting territory already familiar to readers of *The Unlimited Dream Company* (68) and many earlier stories.

The latest Ballard novel is about a man who apparently summons up a great river, becomes obsessed with what he believes to be his creation, and decides to follow it back to its source. At first, the new river seems to spring in miraculous fashion from beneath the stump of an ancient oak, but it soon becomes evident that the life-giving stream is flowing from a mountain chain some 200 miles away (where it has probably been brought into existence by natural causes, a small shift in the earth's crust). The setting of the novel is an imaginary African country, a former French colony which lies to the south of the expanding Sahara desert. The hero, Doctor Mallory, is an Englishman who ostensibly works for the World Health Organization. Mallory's bizarre adventures take place in a part of the world which has become newsworthy of late – we have all seen pictures of starving African populations, and have read of the unending, tragic drought in the Sahel – and indeed the media image of Africa, as projected in hundreds of TV documentaries and nature programmes, is part of the subject–matter of this book. One of the principal European characters, the egregious Professor Sanger, is a television presenter who wishes to make a filmed record of Mallory's crazy quest.

Nevertheless, it is not a 'real' Africa which Ballard gives us. The petty civil war, whose violent see-sawing provides much of the incidental action throughout the story, is unsympathetically portrayed and seems peculiarly point-less. As one might expect, Ballard is not at all interested in the political realities of present–day black Africa. His focus is entirely on the psychology of the individual. This is a first-person narrative, as was *The Unlimited Dream Company*, and for the duration of the novel we are trapped within Mallory's fever-ridden skull as he fights his way upstream, helped by a fey teenage girl and pursued by government soldiers, rebel guerrillas, and a boatload of bereaved women in vengeful mood. The deserts, jungles and lagoons through which they travel are dream-like, landscapes-as-states-of-mind described with all Ballard's usual hallucinatory intensity.

We may read the novel as an allegory of the creative process, a depiction of the love/hate relationship which any creator has with the thing he has created. Mallory's search for the river's source is also a quest for the fount of all inspiration. Given this reading, the closing pages of the book – where the last waters of the river trickle through the hero's fingers – are peculiarly sad, although the sadness is mitigated by a half-promise that the mighty river will one day flow again.

First edition: London, Gollancz, 1987 (hardcover)
First American edition: New York, Farrar, Straus, 1988 (hardcover)
Most recent edition: London, Grafton (paperback)

100

JOHN CROWLEY

Aegypt

Thomas Pynchon's *The Crying of Lot 49* (*31*) was to some
degree a novel about 'the secret history of the world'. The
equally talented John Crowley takes the idea a great deal
further in this, the first volume of a projected four-part
series. His hero, a failed history lecturer called Pierce
Moffett, develops an obsession with the concept of
'Aegypt', a mystical eastern land not at all cognate with the
Egypt of the workaday world. Rooted partly in his childhood fantasies, and partly in the works on alchemy, magic,
astrology and speculative history which he has read, Moffett's Aegypt takes on a mysterious, shimmering reality of
its own. It has no earthly, tangible existence in the novel,
but it is strongly present as a parallel history, a secret story
that has been going on 'for centuries, for all time.' As the
critic Gregory Feeley has succinctly put it, the central theme
of this long fiction is 'the penetration of historiography by
mythopoeia'.

That may sound dry, but in fact the novel is as rich with
emotional life, as humane, as its author's previous magical
opus, *Little, Big* (*76*). As well as the likeably earnest Pierce
Moffett (who resembles Crowley's earlier hero, Smoky
Barnable, in his search for meaning and marriage, and his
removal from the big city to the country) we meet the
attractive Rosie Rasmussen, an inhabitant of the small town
of Blackbury Jambs in the Faraway Hills of New York
State. Rosie is in the throes of divorce, and has a young
child to care for. As an escape from her worries she
immerses herself in the lengthy historical novels written by

a one-time fellow-townsman and deceased relative, Fellowes Kraft. Many of Kraft's tales, from which highly entertaining passages are reproduced in the text, concern the affairs of Dr John Dee, the sage, astrologer and crystallomancer who lived at the time of Queen Elizabeth I. (Dee, a fascinating figure who was perhaps something of a charlatan, also appears in Michael Moorcock's novel *Gloriana*.) Pierce Moffett happens to be familiar with Kraft's novels, and when he comes to live in Blackbury Jambs in order to find the tranquillity to write his proposed book on 'Aegypt', Pierce and Rosie are set on paths which inevitably will cross. So we have the realistic love story of two modern Americans, embedded in a much wider and more complex fiction about history, historical fiction and the hermetic tradition.

Although there is little in the way of conventional mystery-or-fantasy-story excitement, the novel is supremely well written, with scenes of astonishing power and poetry. And though the author does not lend credence to any of the occult mumbo-jumbo from which Pierce has contructed his alternative 'Aegyptian' history (and on which Kraft has built his novels), Crowley's book is nevertheless *about* all that magical lore and its importance to the human imagination. There are hints, in the book's prologue and elsewhere, that the present volume may be subsumed in some wider supernatural scheme of the author's, yet to be revealed. But as Pierce reflects, when he glances through the pages of a meretricious bestseller on the occult tradition: 'Star temples and ley-lines, UFOs and landscape giants, couldn't they see that what was really, permanently astonishing was the human ability to keep finding these things? Let anyone looking for them be given a map of Pennsylvania or New Jersey or the Faraways, and he will find "ley-lines"; let human beings look up long enough on starry nights and they will see faces staring down at them. That's the interesting thing, that's the subject: not why there are ley-lines, but why people find them; not what plan the aliens had for us, but why we think there must, somehow, always have been a plan.' By and large, Crowley brings us back from the fantastic to the mundane in this fine novel; yet, as with the faerie elements in *Little, Big*, the Aegyptology in *Aegypt* serves to heighten the humanity of the story and to enliven us to all the wonders of reality.

First edition: New York, Bantam, 1987 (hardcover)
First British edition: London, Gollancz, 1987 (hardcover)

INDEX